THE WORLD IS
BIGGER NOW

THE WORLD IS
BIGGER NOW

An American Journalist's Release from Captivity in North Korea . . .
A Remarkable Story of Faith, Family, and Forgiveness

❖

Euna Lee

WITH LISA DICKEY

BROADWAY BOOKS
New York

Library of Congress Cataloging-in-Publication Data
Lee, Euna.
The world is bigger now: an American journalist's release from captivity in
North Korea . . . a remarkable story of faith, family, and forgiveness/Euna Lee
with Lisa Dickey. —1st ed.
p. cm.
1. Lee, Euna—Captivity, 2009. 2. Hostages—Korea (North) 3. Journalists—
Korea (North) 4. Americans—Korea (North) 5. Korea (North)—Politics and
government—1994– 6. Journalists—United States—Biography.
I. Dickey, Lisa. II. Title.
PN4874.L364A3 2010
070.92—dc22
[B]   2010019833

ISBN 978-0-307-71613-2

Printed in the United States of America

DESIGN BY AMANDA DEWEY

1 3 5 7 9 10 8 6 4 2

First Edition

For my husband, Michael, who helps me to stand firm in my faith
For my daughter, Hana, who softens my heart
with her carefree heart
And for her brother and sister, who we hope will come. . . .

CONTENTS

THE WORLD IS
BIGGER NOW

OUR LIVES BEFORE, AND A STORY THAT MATTERED

A T AROUND 5 A.M. ON MARCH 17, 2009, the sun had not yet risen over the Tumen River in northeast China. The morning was absolutely still; the only sound I could hear was the rustling of foliage under my feet as I made my way toward the riverbank. I had overslept that morning, so we were running late—we'd have to hurry to get the footage we needed before the sun rose. The Tumen River formed the border between North Korea and China, and it wasn't safe to film there in the daylight when we might be seen.

I had come to the river with my Current TV colleagues Laura Ling and Mitch Koss, as well as a local guide. We'd parked a short distance away, and as we walked from the car to the river's edge, I was already shooting footage for our planned documentary about North Korean defectors. In my viewfinder, with the aid of night vision, I could see Laura and Mitch's feet as they walked across the dry, tangled brush.

No one else was around when we arrived at the river. It was about sixty yards wide, pale blue with ice all the way across, with only brown branches of trees and brush on each side. The still winter air painfully chilled our ears as we looked out over the ice. This could have been any river outside of any town, except that the other side of the water was North Korea.

With its long stretches of uninhabited riverbank, the Tumen was a natural place for North Korean defectors to cross over in search of a better life. Years of famine in North Korea, and the oppressive political situation there, had led hundreds of thousands of people to try to flee the country, and many of them crossed in places just like the one where we now stood. As part of our planned documentary about these defectors, we wanted to show this important route of escape.

Mitch and I would do the filming, and Laura would be in front of the camera, doing the reporting. Our guide, a man in his thirties who had worked with the "underground railroad" support network for defectors, would point out landmarks and suggest places to film.

Just as the sun began to peek over the horizon, our guide, wearing a Chinese police coat he had borrowed from a friend, walked onto the translucent ice. It was absolutely quiet, and I couldn't see movement of any kind on the other side of the river. It was also freezing; stepping onto the ice, I couldn't help but think how cold and frightened anyone trying to cross from the North Korean side would be.

As we followed the guide toward the middle of the river, Mitch said, "Be careful, I hear ice cracking." Mitch was heavier than Laura or me, and he seemed nervous. I was nervous too, but I was mostly focused on getting the best footage we could. We had very limited time in China and South Korea, so we had all been working incredibly hard to get the material we needed for the documentary. Walking on the ice made me nervous, but I figured the guide must know whether it was safe or not. I trusted him.

When we got close to the middle of the river, the guide suddenly began making a low hooting sound. It was a signal of some kind, but for whom? We assumed he must be communicating with the North Korean border guards he knew. We'd heard that some North Korean guards were in contact with people in China, and some had supposedly even spoken to foreign journalists who crossed this same river in search of interviews. We were definitely alert, but not fearful. Not yet.

The guide continued to make hooting sounds, but there was no response from the other side. So he kept going. We followed him, and when we neared the middle of the river, I filmed Laura doing a "standup"—a monologue in which she spoke directly into the camera, describing where we were and how defectors crossed the river. I then shot footage of her walking on the ice as I followed from behind.

We shot another standup so Laura could describe how close the two countries were. But when I paused to show her the digital footage, we realized the shot didn't really show how narrow the river was. "Wait here," I said to Laura. "I'll go back and get a wide shot of you standing on the ice."

But as I started walking back toward the Chinese riverbank, the guide told me to stop. "Don't go back there," he said. "The ice is thin, it might break." The ice didn't seem any thinner there, but the guide insisted and I didn't have time to argue—the sun was coming up and we needed to move fast. So, reluctantly, I walked back to the middle of the river to rejoin the others.

At that point, the guide motioned for us to follow him past the midpoint of the river—and as we crossed into North Korean territory, my heart began to pound. I knew this was a risky move, but I was so intent on getting the story out, I didn't focus on the potential danger. So, at the guide's urging, we followed him farther, all the way to the North Korean riverbank.

He pointed to a small village that looked like it was frozen in time, a collection of five or six huts with thatched roofs. "There," he whispered, pointing.

I zoomed in to where he was pointing, and as I filmed, I knew we were glimpsing an important part of the underground railroad by which thousands of North Koreans have been smuggled into China. This was what we had traveled so far to find, the true story of people putting their lives on the line in a desperate quest for freedom. I felt exhilarated at the sight.

But it was also frightening to be on North Korean soil, so I was relieved when, after only a minute or so, we started back toward the Chinese side. The air was still and everything was quiet—until Mitch's voice suddenly pierced the air. "Run!" he shouted. "Run! Soldiers!" Startled, I turned to see two North Korean soldiers, wearing green military uniforms and holding rifles, sprinting toward us.

Laura, Mitch, the guide, and I all ran toward the Chinese riverbank as fast as we could. I was terrified, running in boots that were too big for me across the slippery ice. It wasn't so much that I was afraid the soldiers would capture me—I was more afraid they would shoot us. A thought flashed into my mind: *If they shoot, maybe the bullets will lodge in my backpack. Please don't let them shoot my head!* Subconsciously, I braced myself for the impact as I ran.

Incredibly, the guide looked over his shoulder and yelled at me, "Are you filming this?" Even more incredibly, after first thinking, *Is he crazy?* I actually pushed the record button and continued to run with the camera pointed back under my arm. Even though I was afraid for my life, I was obsessed with getting good material for the documentary.

Mitch, who was an avid runner and very fast, reached the shore first and disappeared into the bushes. Laura and I also managed to reach Chinese soil, and when we made it to a gravel path by the riverbank, I thought we were safe. Then I saw, just ahead of me, that Laura had fallen—she was on her knees, looking stunned. "Laura!" I shouted. "Are you okay?" Her answer sent a chill through me: "I can't feel my leg."

Seeing that the two soldiers were still coming, the guide reached for my arm. "Let's go! Let's go!" he shouted. "Run!" He yanked me off balance, and I fell, too. Now the soldiers were just steps away, and I looked down at my camera. I thought, *I have to get rid of this!* I knew that when the soldiers saw it, they would realize we had been filming. But there was no time—in an instant, the soldiers had seized us.

Everything happened in a flash. "Give them money!" the guide barked at me. In a daze, I reached into my pocket and took out what I had: 200 Chinese yuan—about $30. But when I handed it to one of the soldiers, he threw it down in disgust.

"Okay, okay, let's talk about this," said the guide, addressing the soldiers in Korean. "Let's all calm down."

"We can talk on our side," one of the soldiers shot back. The guide began to argue with them, then said, "Just take me—let the others go." But the soldiers refused, and when the guide realized he couldn't talk them out of arresting us, he suddenly took off running. One of the soldiers sprinted after him, leaving the other to guard Laura and me. Mitch was nowhere in sight.

The soldier who stayed with us put down his rifle and began to gather our things. "We should grab the gun," Laura whispered. I considered it for a moment but realized I wouldn't know how to use it even if I could get to it. I also considered running—but even if I could outrun this one soldier, Laura couldn't. She was injured, and she couldn't understand anything the Korean soldiers were saying. I wasn't going to leave her.

A minute or two later, the other soldier returned. "That bastard is so fast!" he said. "He got away." He turned his attention to Laura and me. "All right, let's go!" he snapped.

He grabbed Laura, and the other soldier grabbed me, but we both fought back. I latched on to some bushes and wouldn't let go, holding on as tightly as I could. But although the soldiers were small, they were strong. One of them pulled roughly around my waist, pausing only to show me his gun clip and say, "These are real bullets! You need to come with us!"

All I could think was, *You can't do this! We're in Chinese territory!* But the soldier kept yanking at my waist, tearing a belt loop on my pants as he pulled me violently, trying to loosen my grip on the bushes. He kicked me in the shoulders and back, landing blow after blow with his boots. Really scared now, I finally let go of the bushes and wrapped my arms around my head. The soldier grabbed me by the coat and began dragging me toward the river.

"Please let us go!" I cried as he pulled me onto the ice. I tried not to look in his eyes, so as not to anger him. "Please, I'm begging you! Let us go!" But he refused. I desperately tried to grab anything I could, but there was nothing to hold on to.

He kept dragging me, and I kept screaming and begging, hoping someone—anyone—might hear us and come to help.

As the soldier pulled me toward North Korean territory, I suddenly remembered that I had telephone numbers written on a piece of paper in my coat pocket. It was information that, if it fell into North Korean hands, could endanger many people in China and South Korea. So I slipped my arms out of my coat—a warm winter coat my mother had just given me a few days earlier, in Seoul—and left it on the ice. The guard didn't miss a beat, just shifting his grip to my arms and continuing to pull me across the river. Behind us, the other soldier was dragging Laura by her arms, too.

At some point, I came to the terrible realization that there was absolutely no one around who could help us. Mitch was gone, the guide was gone, and we were now more than halfway across the river to North Korea. Exhausted, bruised, and scared, I said to the soldier, "Okay, okay, I'll go! Please don't drag me anymore."

I looked back to where the other soldier was holding Laura and was alarmed to see she was lying facedown on the ice. "Laura!" I yelled. "Are you okay? Wake up!" She lifted her head slowly, seemingly in a daze, and I saw to my horror that blood was streaming down one side of her face. Because we had crossed the line into North Korean territory, my soldier was calmer now, and he waited for his compatriot to drag Laura to where we stood. It was agony watching her being dragged like a rag doll across the ice.

I kept calling to her, but she didn't respond. Finally, when the soldier had dragged her almost to where we stood, I said, "Laura! Reach for my hand!" She lifted her hand to mine and I helped her stand up. "Let's go!" my soldier snapped, and the four of us walked the last fifteen yards to the North Korean riverbank.

"I hope I didn't stop you from running," Laura said weakly. My head was spinning, trying to take in what was happening—but all I could think at that moment was that I didn't want Laura to feel bad on top of everything else.

"It's okay, it was my choice," I told her. "I know you would have done the same. It's better to be two than one." But even as I tried to sound comforting, I was scared out of my wits. As a Christian, I had always believed God would protect me— but where was He now? Why wasn't He helping us?

Ten minutes earlier, I was a free woman, a TV editor shooting a story on my very first overseas assignment. Now I was a captive.

❖

As the soldiers marched us deeper into North Korean territory, the situation felt completely surreal. Just a week and a half earlier, I had been home in Los Angeles with my husband of nine years, Michael Saldate, and our four-year-old daughter, Hana. Now I was in the hands of angry North Korean soldiers, being led like a prisoner into an uncertain future.

The contrast couldn't have been any greater. My life in Los Angeles was safe and predictable. Michael, Hana, and I lived in a comfortable two-bedroom apartment between the affluent neighborhood of Hancock Park and the working-class area known as Korea Town. We'd moved there from North Hollywood six months earlier so Hana would be able to attend a higher-quality elementary school. We loved the family-friendly neighborhood, and Hana was thriving—a happy, bright little preschooler.

Our life at home centered on family and faith. Michael and I had met in San Francisco, where we attended the same church, and he and I shared the belief that our Christian faith would help guide us through good times and bad. Like many young couples, we had occasionally struggled with money issues. We also experienced the usual pressures of having a young child, trying to keep up with her needs and those of the household while making sure our relationship didn't suffer. We worked hard to maintain a balance, and our faith, even if we didn't always succeed.

But no matter what difficulties came up, I always felt lucky to be facing them with Michael. I tend to worry a lot, but whenever I felt anxious, his easygoing nature helped calm me down. He's more of an optimist than I am, always managing to keep up hope and good spirits in the face of hard times. I cherished these traits in him, and sometimes I wished I had more of them in myself.

Michael and I had met and married in San Francisco, and we moved to L.A. in 2007 so he could pursue his lifelong dream of being an actor. At that time, he'd been performing on stage and going to auditions for ten years, but the reality was that there was very little work for actors in the Bay Area. We realized Michael would have a much better chance of getting work in Hollywood, where there are far more roles for actors, so we decided to make the move.

Michael is a natural performer and an extrovert. From the first day we spent time together, back in the summer of 1997, it was obvious that he loved people and had a curious and engaging personality. I'd met Michael once at church, but I didn't really notice him until a mutual friend invited us to see an exhibit of eighteenth-century Korean art in Berkeley one afternoon. We all had bicycles, so we decided to take the BART train and then cycle together to the exhibit.

Art exhibits from different cultures aren't everyone's cup of tea, so I half expected Michael to just wander quickly through the museum and then wait impatiently for us to go. But he was full of questions that day: Why did the artist use this specific technique? How does it work? How does he compare to other Korean artists? Because this particular artist is very famous in South Korea, I had learned about him in high school. So I was able to answer Michael's questions as we walked around together, and the conversation continued afterward, over dinner.

But even before we made it to the exhibit, I'd gotten my first glimpse of Michael's warmth. Two girls, about thirteen years old, had boarded the same BART train we were on, but they seemed lost. Michael asked if they needed help, and he soon figured out that they were on the wrong train. He pointed out each station on their map, patiently explaining how to get to the right one. And until the girls arrived at their stop, he chatted with them and made them feel at ease. He treated these two young strangers like little sisters, and I was touched by his kindness.

Michael's personality was definitely winning. But his clothes, unfortunately, were not. He loved thrift-store paisley shirts and had a collection that looked like it dated from 1978. He also had a pair of sea-green drainpipe pants that he loved dearly—and which I couldn't stand. That, combined with a little goatee, very short hair, and tennis shoes with holes in them, completed a look that wasn't quite what I had in mind for a potential boyfriend. But Michael's charm and warm brown eyes won me over, and I found myself drawn to him. We began dating seriously, and in August 1999 Michael and I were married.

Growing up in Seoul, I had always assumed I'd marry a nice Korean boy, not a handsome American of Mexican descent like Michael. But nothing had gone exactly as planned since I had first come to the United States in 1996, at age twenty-three, to study film editing.

❖

I vividly remember my first day in America—June 3, 1996. As I exited the San Francisco airport with two big black bags, I was wearing blue jeans, my favorite red T-shirt with a dark blue Adidas symbol across the chest, and bright blue sneakers. I went straight to the San Francisco State University campus, dropped my bags off in my new dorm room, and bought a map at the student union. The first thing I wanted to do was visit the Golden Gate Bridge, and I was determined to find my own way there.

With my new map, I managed to catch the number 28 bus and get all the way to the bridge without any help. It was a fantastic summer day, and I was thrilled to see that landmark of San Francisco spanning so majestically across the bay. Excited and wanting to brag to someone, I called my best friend in Korea collect from a pay phone. It was a picture-perfect start to my time in America.

I had come to study a new technique for film editing, the AVID system, which was popular in the United States but not used much yet in South Korea. But although I had studied English in Seoul, there was no way I could understand class lectures on technical subjects without more language instruction. So my plan was to take intensive English-language courses at SFSU, then move on to studying film editing.

My training in film and TV had started at the Seoul Institute of the Arts, where I finished a two-year film-directing program in the early 1990s. This was just a few years after the Berlin Wall collapsed, and it was the tail end of a turbulent time politically in South Korea. Throughout the 1980s, waves of college students had protested what they saw as anti-democratic behavior by the supposedly democratic South Korean government, and when some of the protests turned violent, the government tried to cover up the fact that over time, more than a thousand innocent people were sent to prison for expressing different political views, and many students were killed.

A number of impassioned twenty-something filmmakers, including a group calling itself Arirang (*Ah-ree-rang*), traveled to universities throughout South Korea in the early 1990s, airing controversial films that sought to raise political awareness. One film, titled *Oh! Land of Dreams*, told the story of a massacre in Gwangju city—one of the biggest tragedies in modern South Korean history, and one that the government tried to cover up. In May 1980, students and citizens who had gathered to protest the military dictatorship were brutally attacked by the South Korean army. No one knows the exact numbers, but estimates are that some 200 people were killed and many hundreds more injured. Dozens simply disappeared.

Oh! Land of Dreams was unlike any movie I had ever seen. Arirang opened my eyes to the need to talk about the oppressed, and I saw that film could be a powerful way to do that. I decided I wanted to bring light to the untold stories of people who find themselves in unjust situations. So, during my next two years at the Institute, I created and participated in short films that told the stories of people on the fringes of society—people like a mother whose child died in a fire because, without any government program to aid her, she couldn't afford day care and had to leave him at home while she worked. Making these short films was my way of giving a voice to the voiceless, and I wanted to continue doing it.

Despite where my heart was, I also had to deal with the difficult reality of finding work, and my first two jobs after graduation were working with well-known South Korean commercial film and TV directors. Neither job offered me the chance to tell the stories of the oppressed, but I continued to learn the behind-the-scenes process of making movies. I was fascinated by all the decisions that go into making a film—choosing the angles of a shot, laying out the scenes, and editing everything together to tell a story.

Then one day an assistant director asked me to help make a trailer for a TV series. I couldn't wait to test my skills! I carefully chose shots and edited them together to make the first twenty seconds of the trailer, and the end result was, I thought, pretty good. But it wasn't just me who thought so—the executive producer happened to stop by the edit room and really loved what I'd done, too.

That was the moment I realized I wanted to be an editor. I had studied directing, but being a director is a very difficult job—not only do you have to know a little bit of everything in the field, but you also have to lead the crew. I've never been the kind of person to stand in front of a crowd and take charge; I'm more comfortable dealing with people one-on-one, preferably behind the scenes.

As an editor, I would still get to shape the story but wouldn't have to deal with a lot of people—it was the perfect job for me. Now I just needed to make myself the best editor I could possibly be. Learning AVID in the United States was my first step toward doing that, after which I planned to return to South Korea to continue my career in film. But my relationship with Michael changed all that. Although he loved South Korea when he traveled there, our home was in America. And though I had always planned to move back, I found myself happy to stay in California.

While studying at SFSU, I applied and was accepted at the Academy of Art University in San Francisco, and I started classes there in January 1997. Though my English had improved, I still had trouble understanding everything my instructors said—but even so, I worked hard and was able to create good projects. By the end of my first semester, I felt sure I had chosen the right career path, and the encouragement I received from my teachers further convinced me.

In the summer of 2000, I was eight months away from graduation and had been married to Michael for nearly a year. I'd been working as an intern at Tech TV, a cable and satellite channel that covered technology, and hoping a full-time job would open up there. Eventually, when an assistant editor position opened up, I jumped at the chance to apply for it.

This was it, my dream job—the perfect entry-level position for a fledgling editor.

On the morning of my interview, I stared at the clothes in my closet. What should I wear? A suit? Or something more casual? I decided on a pair of funky silver vinyl pants and platform shoes, hoping to make an impression, and I felt good walking in for the interview. Waiting to hear whether I got the job was agonizing, but finally the call came: I was hired! This was the beginning of my career in editing, and I couldn't wait to get started.

For the next three and a half years, I learned everything I could—from working with tapes to digitizing to editing—while working with the professionals at Tech TV. My skills were growing, but unfortunately, in May 2004, almost everyone was laid off when Tech TV merged with Comcast's G4 channel. But with so many big life changes, an event that first seems terrible might also offer opportunity—something my mom had often told me when I was growing up.

My job at Tech TV was gone, and now I really wanted to think about what I would do next. I had been so focused on simply finding work in my field, forever looking ahead rather than around me, that I had forgotten my original purpose in getting into filmmaking. I knew editing was the perfect job for me, but now I was seeking something larger: Was there some way I could use my skills for a greater purpose?

Although I was pregnant with Hana by then, I was anxious to get back to work. The truth is, I'd never seen myself as a housewife or stay-at-home mom. I wanted to be a career woman. Hana was born in October of 2004, and I took just one month off before starting a contract job at TV station KTSF. Luckily, Michael was able to care for Hana enough days that I could continue doing the work I loved.

Then, in the summer of 2005, I interviewed for a position at a new network cofounded by former Vice President Al Gore. Current TV was planned as an independent alternative to traditional cable channels like CNN and MTV, with a twist. Not only would Current show professionally produced content, it would show short user-generated clips, too. But the network's bread and butter was documentaries—a genre I been trying, but so far unable, to break into.

My goal had always been to edit feature films, but there's a real art to cutting a great documentary—both depend on good storytelling. When it turned out that Current was hiring editors, it seemed the timing was perfect. I could learn a lot there, and I pushed hard to win the position. When they offered me a job in July 2005, four weeks before the network officially launched, I eagerly accepted.

For the first few weeks, everyone worked around the clock in preparation for the launch. Current had hired five editors, and four of us were new to their editing system, so we had to learn it as we went along. I did finishing work—things like cleaning up colors and sound quality—and although it wasn't terribly creative, the adrenaline rush of launching a new network carried me through. We were so proud when

Current finally went on the air! But after the launch, when the excitement died down, I set my sights on finding better, more interesting projects at the network.

Vanguard, the team that made original documentaries for Current, was where I wanted to be. Editing is fun and rewarding, but when I saw the material Vanguard was producing, I knew it would be rewarding on a whole different level. The documentaries Vanguard had planned were about people who were forgotten or ignored by other news outlets. They told stories that could help people—giving voices to the voiceless, just as Arirang had done. Working with this team at Current TV would be both professionally challenging and personally fulfilling—a way to do more than just make a living. It would be a way to give back.

Yet it wouldn't be accurate to say I was driven only by a desire to give back. I was also driven by a work ethic instilled in me by my parents. When I was growing up in South Korea, my parents always worked hard to give us a comfortable life. But although my childhood photos capture cozy family scenes—my father teaching us to ice-skate, my parents taking us to the park, the truth is, I have very few memories of real bonding time with either my mother or my father. They were too busy worrying about money to really be present for my sisters and me.

Without realizing it, I was completely absorbing the belief that success brings happiness. That was the model I saw in my parents, and it was the model I ended up following. I just kept working harder and harder, convinced deep down that if I could make a certain amount of money or achieve a certain social status, my family would be happy. What I didn't ever notice was that the pursuit itself was actually robbing us of happiness, as my ambitions—and my stress level—rose.

I tried hard to get into Vanguard but was frustrated time and again. Either there wasn't an opening, or the timing didn't work out—there was always some reason I couldn't make the switch. But in the meantime, I did some project work for the team, editing mini documentaries. Vanguard produced a lot of these, so I was glad to be able to help out—and hopeful that doing so would get my foot in the door.

One day, a producer in the acquisition department asked me to cut an hour-long documentary called *Seoul Train* down to ten minutes for broadcast. I didn't know it at the time, but his request would change my life. What was meant to be a routine work project triggered the series of events that eventually culminated in my capture at the frozen Tumen River, more than five thousand miles away from my comfortable life in California.

❉

Seoul Train follows three groups of North Korean defectors who have made it halfway to freedom: They've managed to escape from North Korea into China, but they're still at great risk, because Chinese authorities will send them back if they can catch them. And according to North Korean law, any defector who is returned there faces prison, labor camp, or even execution.

North Korea is bordered on the north by China (and a small sliver of Russia), on the south by South Korea, and on the east and west by bodies of water. Because the border with South Korea is so heavily fortified, the only real option for most defectors is to flee into China. But once in China, the North Koreans must stay in hiding until they can find their way to a more refugee-friendly country, such as Thailand or Mongolia.

In keeping with international law, China is supposed to provide safe haven for North Korean refugees. According to the United Nations definition, a refugee is a person who has "a well-founded fear of being persecuted for reasons of race, religion, nationality, [or] membership of a particular social group or political opinion." A refugee is also a person who, because of fear, is "unwilling to avail himself of the protection of that country . . . [or] unwilling to return to it."

But despite protests by human rights groups, the Chinese government is still sending North Koreans back, where they are brutally punished or killed. The Chinese consider these North Koreans to be illegal economic migrants rather than political refugees. And because the Chinese government has close ties with North Korea, it is less interested in protecting the rights of defectors than in keeping the North Korean government happy. Even if that means committing innocent people to prison, or to death.

Seoul Train was made to shed light on the terrible practice of sending refugees back. By some estimates, as many as 300,000 North Korean refugees are hiding in China. But labeling them "refugees" or "defectors" doesn't really tell their story. These are people like you and me, ordinary men and women and families who just want to live with the basic human rights everyone deserves. In *Seoul Train*, we meet these people and get to know them, before watching in horror as some of them try, and fail, to make that final step to freedom.

The footage in *Seoul Train* is wrenching. I watched, riveted, as a smiling young woman named Nam Chun-mi described her desire to live in freedom. Eight and a half months pregnant, she was part of a group of twelve North Koreans who tried to cross from China into Mongolia using fake Chinese ID cards. All twelve were arrested at the border, and only two—a mother and her teenage daughter—were released. The other ten, including Nam Chun-mi, were forcibly returned to North Korea. Her fate is unknown, but she is almost certainly either in prison or dead.

Another family of five made a desperate dash for the safe haven of the Japanese consulate in Shenyang, China. As hidden cameras across the street captured the scene, the young parents, uncle, and grandmother of a two-year-old girl named Han-mi tried to rush through the gate with her. The men made it through, but Chinese guards tackled Han-mi's mother and grandmother, and the little girl, her hair in pigtails, stood watching nearby in fear as the guards wrestled them roughly to the ground.

Fortunately, the story of Han-mi's family had a happy ending. When the shocking footage of their arrest was publicized, there was an international outcry. China bowed to pressure and released the family, allowing them safe passage to South Korea. But I couldn't forget their desperate dash for freedom, and the heartbreaking confusion on little Han-mi's face. She was only a little older than Hana at the time, so these scenes really affected me. After watching *Seoul Train*, I went home that evening and said to Michael, "We have to do something to help these people."

The truth was, I had never really thought about the plight of North Koreans. Growing up in postwar South Korea, we were taught in school that North Koreans were bad people and their government was evil. I had never considered the fact that we were all fellow Koreans, with centuries of shared cultural history, despite the differences of our governments. But watching the people in *Seoul Train*—hearing them speak my native language and describe their hopes and dreams of freedom that I have taken for granted—really opened my eyes.

Yet although I felt moved by the documentary, there wasn't much Michael and I could do at the time to help. Our lives were a whirlwind of trying to pay the bills, take care of Hana, and balance our work and relationship. The more hours I put in at Current, the less time Michael and I had for ourselves—and because I was terrible at promoting myself, it seemed as though the work I was putting in went mostly unnoticed. I was frustrated, and falling deeper into the trap of always feeling like I needed to just work a little harder, a few more hours here and there, to get to whatever goal I'd set. The problem was, every time I reached one goal, there was another one just beyond it.

Then, to add even more stress to the situation, Michael and I decided in 2007 to go ahead and make the move to Los Angeles. Fortunately, Current was able to offer me a position in their L.A. office—but it was for much less interesting work than my position in San Francisco. I wanted Michael to be happy and have a real chance to make it as an actor, so I was willing to take that step for him. But after we made the move, I became more determined than ever to earn a spot on the Vanguard team—which meant even more hours at work, more effort, and more stress.

The person who could help me make the switch was Mitch Koss. Mitch had been in the TV news business since 1983, and he had traveled the world making documentaries. He was credited with helping develop a young Anderson Cooper after the two met in the mid-1990s, and he had also worked with Laura Ling's older sister, Lisa, who went on to become well known as a cohost of *The View*. Lisa and Mitch had traveled together to Afghanistan and Pakistan in the 1990s. And now Mitch was working with Laura at Vanguard.

When I told Mitch how much I wanted to join the Vanguard team, he gave me a project to work on—a one-hour documentary about the state of nuclear proliferation in the world, and what the UN's watchdogs were doing about it. This was an unpaid tryout, and for the next six weeks I worked my normal eight-hour days, then hurried home to put in hours more work on the documentary. It was stressful and tiring, but when I brought Mitch the finished product in less than two months, he was impressed. He offered me another project—this one with pay. I would work for the Vanguard team three days a week and my old position the other two days.

This was it—I had finally gotten my foot in the door! Mitch assigned me to work on a documentary about the island of Saipan, and then one about parolees to be titled *Getting Out of Prison*. Laura Ling was the correspondent on that one, so I went out with her and Mitch to do some shooting as second camera. This marked the first time that Laura, Mitch, and I had ever worked together. I still wasn't a full-time member of the Vanguard team, but I hoped that transition would come soon.

By the fall of 2008, Michael, Hana, and I were settling into Los Angeles, and I was working as hard as ever. Things were going well, though we continued to face the challenges of balancing work and home life as Hana grew into an ever-more-active little girl. Then, one morning in mid-November, I got a call from a colleague at Current.

"Are you okay?" he asked.

"Yes, I'm fine," I said. "What do you mean? Did something happen?"

He told me that Current had been hit with double-digit layoffs—sixty employees in all—so he was checking to make sure I was still on staff. I was, though it turned out that my two-day-a-week position had been eliminated. But with the restructuring, there was now space for me to move to Vanguard full-time. In a bittersweet stroke of luck, the layoffs made it possible for me to take the position I had been fighting for all along.

A couple of weeks later, as I settled into my new position at Vanguard, Mitch approached me with a proposal. "We're planning to make a documentary about North Korean defectors," he told me. "Can you do some research on it?" I was excited to have the opportunity to work on a story that had moved me so much.

It was as if everything had come full circle. This was my chance to make a difference, to help the people whose stories had moved me so much. I couldn't wait to get started.

Two

NO MIDDLE GROUND

Throughout December and into January 2009, I researched the plight of North Korean refugees. I desperately wanted to do a great job, so I immersed myself completely in work, becoming even more distant from Michael and Hana.

In early January, Mitch asked if I wanted to come to South Korea and China with him and Laura to film there. I was really excited and ready to jump at the chance. But traveling to Asia would mean being separated from Michael and Hana for more than two weeks. Not only had I never been away from Michael for that long, I had spent only one night away from Hana. This would be an amazing professional opportunity—Mitch was going to credit me as a co-producer on the project—but what would it mean for our family life?

I always tried to be the best mother I could, but the truth was, when I got pregnant I wasn't sure Michael and I were ready, emotionally or financially, to have a baby. Unlike many expectant mothers, I didn't feel fulfilled and excited—I mostly just felt nauseated and inconvenienced. I worried that maybe we were starting our family too soon, that maybe I wasn't yet cut out to be a mom.

On the day Hana was born, I got only a brief glimpse of her before the doctors whisked her away. I'd had a fever during labor, and when she finally came out, the doctors did a few quick tests and took her immediately to the intensive care unit—I didn't even get to hold her that day. Then we got the news: Hana's pulmonary vein was attached to the wrong atrium in her heart. She would need surgery.

She was so tiny—just under seven pounds. How could she possibly endure open-heart surgery? The next day, I told Michael I needed to see her. I was exhausted and weak from the labor and delivery, but the motherly instinct I wasn't sure I had suddenly kicked in. He held me by the arm and walked me slowly down to the neonatal intensive care unit, and as I looked at little Hana lying there amid tubes and machines, I felt a rush of love—and guilt.

I had been so focused on my work during my pregnancy—in pushing myself to the limit, had I somehow done harm to Hana? Over all those months, I had never slowed down, never stopped to think about how the stresses of my job might affect her. Now, whether it was true or not, I worried that my baby was ill because of my choices. So I made up my mind to do everything I could for her now that she was born. I pumped breast milk and brought it down to the ICU to feed her, sat next to her while she slept, and sang gospel songs I used to listen to during my pregnancy. And I prayed.

For that first week, I was practically living in the ICU, getting only about three hours of sleep a night. But I spent as much time as I could with Hana, because the doctors had advised us to go ahead with her surgery as soon as possible. Winter was coming, and if we postponed the surgery, we'd have to keep her warm at all times so as not to overwork her heart.

Hana had the first of two surgeries just seven days after she was born. Fortunately, everything went smoothly and she recovered very well. But from then on, I was incredibly protective of her, even more so than most first-time mothers. She began walking late, at almost sixteen months, and I was always afraid she would fall and hurt herself. When she began running, I would stand close by, ready to catch her if she stumbled. Despite the fact that I wanted her to grow up into a confident and independent young woman, I couldn't help but baby her.

And Hana seemed perfectly happy to be her mother's baby. She doesn't mind being taken care of, and she is much more easygoing than I am. Like Michael, she enjoys teasing people and has a vivid imagination. She's also unusually sensitive, and she gets upset if someone is hurt or sad—even if they're playacting. But most of the time, she's just a happy kid, full of smiles and mischief, content with her place in the world.

As much as I love Hana, Michael has always been the real emotional rock for her. Our roles are reversed from the typical husband-wife, father-mother roles. I was always the one who worried about providing financially for the family, since my career as a film editor brought in more income than Michael's jobs. And Michael is more naturally nurturing than I am, a steady and comforting presence for both Hana and me. Whenever situations arose where I could make more money for us, I always took the extra work and Michael picked up the slack at home. It seemed to make the most sense for all of us, but it was also a legacy of the Korean mentality I had seen in my parents—that providing financially for your family is a way of nurturing them.

Going to Asia with Mitch and Laura wouldn't bring us more money, but it would help me solidify my position at Vanguard, while offering a way to shed light on an incredibly important story. I knew I wanted to do it as soon as Mitch offered, but I needed to check with Michael first.

That evening at home, I told Michael about Mitch's offer. "I really want to do this story," I told him. "But you'd be alone with Hana for two and a half weeks. I know it's a lot to ask—"

"Honey," he interjected, "this is a great opportunity. I'm

excited for you!" He smiled in that warm, caring way that had won me over a decade earlier. "Go ahead, do the story. And do your best." I felt lucky to have such a husband at that moment—not for the first time, and certainly not for the last.

I dove back into my research on North Korean refugees, and the more I learned, the more outrageous it all seemed. I had been moved by the stories of the few dozen people in *Seoul Train*. But that handful of refugees was just the tip of the iceberg: Day after day, month after month, thousands of North Koreans risked their lives to escape the oppression and poverty in their country. Realizing how many people were living in daily fear in China, or being captured and sent back to punishment, was overwhelming.

In the course of my research, I also learned about the network of people who worked in secret to help North Korean refugees. This "underground railroad" was spread out across China and South Korea, and the people in it worked tirelessly to bring defectors to safety, sometimes putting themselves at great risk to do so: In China, a person caught having contact with North Korean defectors can be sentenced to ten years in prison. It was inspiring to learn about their devotion to the cause, and I began to feel not only a professional obligation to tell the story, but a personal one, too.

Then, early one morning in mid-January, I got a call from someone in Seoul whom I'd spoken with several times in the course of my research. He told me he was communicating via Internet video chat with a young defector in China. "He's being held in a guarded room on the seventh floor of a building, but he's going to try to escape through a window," the man told me. "You can open up a video chat on your computer, interview him, and film him trying to escape."

This was the real thing, a defector trying to make it to freedom, and I had a chance to get it on film! What did I need to do to make this happen? I didn't have a camera at home, so I'd need to rush to work to get one. But suddenly, I remembered what day it was—I had jury duty in downtown L.A. that morning, and had already postponed it twice. I couldn't postpone it again, and not showing up would result in a fine or worse.

Was there any other way to get the footage? I considered calling Mitch to ask him to film the defector. But Mitch didn't speak Korean, so he wouldn't be able to communicate with him. All these thoughts raced through my head, and I realized with dismay that there was no way to make it work.

"I'm so sorry," I told the man after a moment's hesitation. "I really want to do this, but I just can't this morning." I asked whether the defector would be okay, and the man said he didn't know. Reluctantly, I hung up the phone.

For days after this incident, I felt terrible. How dedicated was I, really, as a journalist? Half a world away, people were risking their lives for freedom, and I couldn't even spare the time to help bring their stories to life? *Am I cut out for this?* I wondered. *Did I make the right decision?* From that moment, I couldn't stop thinking about the young man on the seventh floor.

Filled with guilt, I knew I needed to work harder than ever to get the best possible material for our documentary.

❖

Laura, Mitch, and I were scheduled to fly to Seoul on March 9, so I didn't have much time to finish my research, arrange contacts and interviews in South Korea and China, and otherwise prepare for my first overseas assignment. I would have four jobs—as producer, camerawoman, interpreter, and editor. With all that responsibility, my stress level was increasing even as my excitement grew.

About a week before the trip, our church was hosting a weekend picnic. We were pretty new to the church, and as always I didn't really look forward to meeting new people, but Michael and Hana were excited about it, so we decided to go.

Throughout the afternoon, I wasn't really there. I pushed Hana in a swing and watched her playing with other kids, and I saw Michael chatting with people, but my mind was elsewhere. There was so much to do before I left, so many details to tie up, that I couldn't relax and enjoy this time with my family. It wasn't just organizing for the trip that I was worrying about. It was important to me to prepare Hana for how long I would be gone.

One evening the same week, Hana and I went up to her room after dinner and sat down together on her bed. I pointed to the Barbie calendar above her headboard and made her a promise. "See this day, Hana?" I asked. "This is the day when Mommy goes to work. And this day here"—I pointed to March 26—"is the day Mommy will come home." Together, she and I marked the seventeen days on her calendar.

When I'd first told Hana I would be away for that long, she was upset. She started to cry, and as I tried to comfort her, I asked what I could bring her from Korea. She answered right away, "A swan princess dress?" She'd been watching the animated movie *The Swan Princess*, and the idea of getting her own dress brightened her right up. Since then, she had seemed to accept that I'd be away, and I was comforted by the thought that her regular schedule and routine would help things to feel normal for her in my absence.

I was scheduled to leave on a Monday, and normally Michael would have been home all weekend, meaning we'd get to spend time together. But that weekend, he was in Fresno from Friday through Sunday morning, spending two nights there for a shoot. And when he got back on Sunday, he had two auditions on opposite sides of L.A., so we spent most of the day in the car. As much as I tried to be brave and go about planning for my trip as if it was just "business as usual," I felt like I missed him already. And with so much left to do before leaving the next morning, my stress level kept rising.

That night, I was putting together a photo book for my parents, whom I was planning to see in Seoul. I was trying to do it quickly, but Hana wanted to help.

"I want to put some pictures in, Mommy!" she said. I handed her a picture, but her little hands were clumsy and, as she tried to put it in the book, she accidentally ripped a page. The first time it happened, I didn't say anything. But when she ripped another page, I snatched the book from her hand.

Instead of explaining that I was in a hurry, or telling her she could help next time, I silently pasted the photos in myself. "Why won't you let me do it?" she asked me, hurt. "I want to help." But I just ignored her question, unwilling to get in a conversation about it when I had so little time. It was a moment that would come to haunt me while I was in captivity in North Korea.

The next morning, Michael's plans to drive me to the airport were interrupted when he got a call for a temp job. He left the house early, leaving me to finish up last-minute packing and get Hana to school. We had a hurried good-bye, and I said, "See you in a couple of weeks!" I think we both figured the time would fly by and I'd be home before we knew it.

In her bedroom, Hana wanted to put on her favorite dress for school, a short-sleeved, knee-length dress with light purple flowers. I pulled it over her head, but when I started to button it up in the back, I noticed one button was missing.

"Hana, I can see your skin!" I told her. "Your dress is missing a button."

"That's okay!" she said. "I want to wear it anyway." Hana really loved this dress, and on this morning of all mornings, I wasn't about to make her change out of it.

It was a twenty-minute walk to Hana's preschool, where she learns Korean culture and language, and usually we walked straight there to save time. But Hana loves to play, and today she wanted to play the "catch me" game. She ran ahead of me, hiding behind bushes or around corners and shouting, "Catch me!" I would find her and act surprised, and she'd laugh and run ahead again. We had such a nice walk, I was sorry when we finally reached her school.

"I'll be back soon," I told her, bending down to hug her. She just kissed me on the cheek, chirped "Bye!," and then turned to run to her class. I was glad she was okay, but a little disappointed we hadn't had more of a moment together. As I watched her disappear into the building, I noticed the missing button again and wondered what her teacher would think. What kind of mother would send her daughter to school dressed like that?

❖

Our flight to Seoul took about two extra hours because of tensions that had flared between North and South Korea earlier that week. The government in Seoul had announced that it would hold joint military exercises with the United States, which the government in Pyongyang considered a threat. The North Koreans had warned that they would shoot at any aircraft encroaching on their airspace, so commercial airlines were making sure to route their flights well away from North Korean territory.

I took advantage of the flying time to do some more research. I'd brought along articles and reports to read, and spent the hours in flight poring over them and taking notes. It's not unusual for me to get carried away when I work, forgetting about everything else, and that's exactly what had happened in the days leading up to the trip. I usually turned to God when things were difficult, and sometimes forgot about Him when things were going well. I had forgotten to ask God for guidance and help on this trip, and even now, on the plane hurtling toward South Korea, I was still too caught up in work to remember.

When we finally arrived in Seoul, I was tired from the long flight but also excited, because two of my best friends from college were coming to visit me at our hotel that evening. I hadn't seen Su-yun and Eun-Kyoung since Michael and I came to South Korea for Su-yun's wedding in 2003, and they came bearing all kinds of gifts—food, an umbrella, sweaters, warm socks. We stayed up talking until about 2 A.M., and made plans to meet again before I headed back to Los Angeles. It was a wonderful start to what I knew would be a grueling work trip.

The next morning, Laura, Mitch, and I got right to work. We had only two days in Seoul and one week in China to shoot all the material we needed, as Laura and Mitch were returning to L.A. on March 20. I'd be staying in Seoul for another week to visit family and friends, and possibly shoot more if needed, but our goal was to get enough footage for an hour-long documentary in those nine days. So we definitely had our work cut out for us.

Our first stop was the office of a preacher, Pastor Chun, who was active in the Korean underground railroad. Pastor Chun was the closest thing the movement had to a celebrity. He offered himself up as its public face, and while many of those who helped North Korean defectors attempted to disguise their identities, Pastor Chun was quick to offer quotes and interviews on camera. Any story about North Korean defectors usually brought some involvement with—or mention of—him and his church, and ours was no different.

I had spoken with Pastor Chun several times while doing research in L.A., and he had invited us to come meet some defectors at his office in Seoul. Laura, Mitch, and I took a taxi across town, and although Pastor Chun wasn't there, we met two young men who had escaped several years earlier from North Korea. Both agreed to be interviewed, on the condition that we not show their faces on camera.

I set up my camera to film the first man, focusing only on his mouth to protect his identity, and he began to tell us his story. Like most defectors, he had escaped from North Korea by sneaking across the Tumen River into China. But at that point he wasn't yet free, as Chinese authorities would return him to North Korea if they could find him. He knew he had to make it to another country, or at least some neutral political ground within China, to gain his freedom.

He talked it over with a friend, and the two of them decided to seek protection on the grounds of a German school not far from where they were hiding. He'd have to scale the fence surrounding the school—and he had to do it quickly, or Chinese guards would catch and arrest him. He chose his day and time, and the attempt was videotaped. We watched the clip with him that morning in Pastor Chun's office.

On the video, we could see two young men wearing shorts and collared shirts, filmed from behind. The camera follows as they race to the top of a staircase leading to a metal door—an emergency gate of some sort—in an effort to out-run the Chinese authorities. Watching them rush to safety reminded me of the scenes I'd watched in *Seoul Train* where men and women scrambled over and through fences in a desperate quest to escape.

"What were you thinking at the time?" Laura asked him.

"It was very intense," he said. "It was life or death. If they caught me, I'd get sent back. I could imagine killing anyone who tried to stop me." It was hard to conceive of facing that one moment that could save your life—or possibly end it. There was no middle ground.

The second man was a little older than the first, but still in his twenties. He told us he had escaped North Korea repeatedly, as Chinese authorities had captured him several times and sent him back. I was amazed to hear that he'd managed to escape more than once from North Korean labor camps to which he'd been sentenced, as these camps are very heavily guarded and usually in remote locations. When I asked how he did it, he would only say, "It's a long story."

As we were talking, the man's phone rang. After a brief conversation, he hung up and told us it was his aunt calling—from North Korea. We were astonished. Most North Koreans had no contact with South Korea, as there were no landline phone connections outside of North Korea and no cell phones for ordinary North Koreans. But his aunt had a contraband cell phone, smuggled in from China. Even so, it wasn't easy to get a signal; typically, North Koreans with cell phones had to go over the tops of hills near the Chinese border to pick up signals there, as there were no cell phone towers in North Korea. She had a phone plan through a Chinese carrier, and arrangements had been made for someone there to pay the bill.

We asked the man if we could film him calling his aunt, and he agreed. He tried three times and couldn't get through, but on the fourth try, she answered. I had connected an earphone to my camera, so I was able to hear both ends of the conversation.

The first thing I noticed was the distinctive way she spoke Korean—her accent was very different from those of South Koreans, and even different from that of the North Koreans we'd met here, who were trying to assimilate into South Korea. She asked him to send money and told him things had been hard lately. He told her he couldn't, because he didn't earn enough to spare any. Their conversation was short, but I could hear the desperation in her voice.

I could also sense his frustration. After hanging up, he told me, "It's not so easy to save money for them. They think it's easy, but they have no idea what it's like living in a capitalist country." His words served as a reminder that, even when North Koreans make it to freedom, life doesn't suddenly become easy for them. They have to make a transition to a completely different way of life.

In all my research, I'd never heard of anyone being able to call from South Korea to North Korea. But something else about their conversation surprised me just as much.

"How do you send money to someone in North Korea?" I asked the man. It's not like other countries, where you can just make a deposit or wire transfer, after all.

He said that if you have an account in China, you can send money to North Korea. He meant that enough people cross secretly back and forth between the two countries that you can send money with them. It was also rumored that North Korean border guards could be bribed, which was another possible way to get money across the border. But these were both extreme scenarios—hardly anyone traveled between the two countries, because the risk was so great.

With the whole world being so interconnected, it's strange to think of how isolated North Korea really is. Most North Koreans have no idea what the Internet is and have never seen Hollywood movies, which are banned by the government because, it is claimed, they promote capitalist ideas. They also don't realize how unusual it is that the vast majority of their country—as widely publicized nighttime satellite images have shown—has little to no electricity. It's as though they live in a tightly sealed box, with only rumors of what the rest of the world might be like.

We couldn't help but wonder, too, about the North Koreans' feelings for their "Dear Leader," Kim Jong-il. In the West, he is usually portrayed as eccentric and egotistical, a man more interested in holding on to power than making sure his people have enough food. But in North Korea, the state-run media portray him as a near-deity.

Laura asked the first defector, "Do people really respect Kim Jong-il?" He responded that people loved the previous leader, Kim Jong-il's father, Kim Il-sung. But, he went on, ever since the son came to power and the famines started, people were only pretending to respect him.

Kim Jong-il became the leader of North Korea in 1994, after the death of his father, and the country suffered terrible flooding the next year, followed by droughts in the late 1990s that decimated the food supply. According to most estimates, between two and three million North Koreans died during the famines, a period referred to there as "the arduous march." The defector described for us the discontent many people seemed to feel in North Korea—discontent that the government would never acknowledge.

We wrapped up the interviews and thanked both defectors for letting us film them. It was only our first day, but I was excited that we'd already gotten so much good material. I hoped it was a sign of things to come.

Next, Mitch, Laura, and I caught a taxi to Imjingak, a park near the border with North Korea. Imjingak, which has several monuments commemorating the Korean War, is one of the most popular places for South Koreans to look across at the North Korean side. It's a place where people can come and simply contemplate, or perhaps feel some connection with loved ones on the other side of the border.

The drive from Seoul took just under an hour, and the closer we got, the more signs we saw of military activity. Jets were flying overhead, tanks were rumbling along the road. The tensions between North and South Korea were still high because of the incident earlier in the week, and both sides were making a show of military strength. It made the trip to the border feel that much more intense.

At the park, there's a chain-link fence where people can tie pieces of cloth with messages for those on the other side, or notes expressing hopes for reunification. Though they'll never make it to their intended recipients, the notes are a way for people to express their feelings and leave a memento. We looked at a few, including a heartbreaking one that said, "I miss you, Mom. I hope to see you soon."

It was strange to stand behind a fence and look over at North Korea. We could see the mountains just across the border, and although they looked peaceful, we heard gunshots coming from the North Korea side—more military maneuvers. And there were railroad tracks, where a train used to run from South Korea to North Korea. Just looking at those tracks made me feel solemn about the sixty years of separation between the two countries. North Korea was so close, and yet farther away than any other place we could reach.

We filmed some standups at the park with Laura, and I shot some B-roll footage that we could intersperse throughout the documentary. On the way back to Seoul, we stopped at a stretch of the Imjin River, which flows between North and South Korea. A fence had been erected along the walk to the river, and I noticed there were little rocks suspended between the fence's wires. This seemed strange, so I asked the taxi driver how the rocks got there.

"In old times," he said, "the spies from the north would cut the fence to come over. Cutting it would loosen the fence, and rocks would fall when they shook it. That's how the authorities can tell that someone has been there." Ever since the Korean War, spies have crossed regularly between North and South Korea, and this was a primitive tactic for finding out who'd been poking around at the border. It was just another reminder that the two countries were still technically at war.

That afternoon, we went to Pastor Chun's church just outside Seoul, where we were hoping to film a service and interview more defectors. It had already been a long day, but we needed to take every chance we could to get good material, so Laura, Mitch, and I positioned ourselves around the room, ready to capture the service.

The two men we'd interviewed earlier that day were there, so I began shooting some B-roll of them, taking care not to film their faces. That's when I noticed a girl nearby. She was crying, very emotional, and I wondered whether she was a defector, too. I took a brief shot from the side and saw that she continued to cry throughout the service. In fact, many people started getting emotional, and I could sense the congregation's feelings intensifying as I continued to film.

The emotion in the room started getting to me, and soon I felt overcome by the stories of what the North Koreans had gone through—all the suffering and uncertainty they had endured in their search for freedom, which they finally attained when they stepped on South Korean soil. As Mitch and Laura continued to shoot on the other side of the room, I sat in a corner and wept. I was embarrassed to be crying while working, something I'd never done before. But as I looked at the faces of the men and women at the church service, it was as if I could feel the hardship they had been through.

❈

The next morning, Laura, Mitch, and I got right back to work. We met with a young woman in her twenties, now a student, whom I'll call Kay. She had defected a few years earlier, and her story sounded like a movie—full of drama, emotion, and twists—but it was all too real.

Kay was pretty, with big dark eyes, short hair, and stylish clothes, and she was able to blend in perfectly in South Korea. She had been working as a bookkeeper at a company in North Korea, making a low wage, when someone she knew came to her and said, "Why don't you go to China? You'd make more money and could learn new computer programs. Just go for two years, and then you can come back." There were contacts who could help her—people who would pick her up on the China side and help her get started there.

She was tempted, as her mother was sick and they never seemed to have enough money for food and medicine. It would be risky, of course—but if she could make good money and come back in just two years, wouldn't that be worth it? She had always been interested in computers, too, so this would be a good chance to learn some new skills. She decided to do it, and began making plans.

When all the arrangements were in place, Kay made her way to the Tumen River. It wasn't winter, so there was no ice to run across—she'd have to wade and, if necessary, swim. But the current was very fast, and she was only five feet tall and about 100 pounds. There was no other way to get to China, though, so in the pitch black of night, carrying her clothes in a plastic bag to keep them dry, she plunged into the river. Very quickly, she found herself up to her neck in the swirling water and scared to death.

She managed to fight her way across, and when she pulled herself onto the Chinese shore, she quickly put on her dry clothes—common practice for defectors, as walking around in dripping wet clothes near the river would raise suspicions if anyone saw them. Someone was waiting there for Kay, and because everything had been arranged beforehand, she readily got into the car. But the driver took her to a nearby town, walked her into a building, and locked her in a room. Yes, she would be working in China—but not at the kind of job she expected.

Kay was too embarrassed to tell us exactly what she did while in China, but I knew from my research what happened to many North Korean women in her situation. They were forced to become Internet sex workers—women who appeared on video in paid online chat rooms. These women were forced to spend hours on end, locked in small rooms, engaging in sex chat with—and sometimes undressing in front of the camera for—men who paid for their services. Because they were in China illegally, these women had no real recourse and nowhere to go. They were captives.

It's hard to imagine how frightening and demeaning this is. My heart swelled for Kay as she told her story of being held captive in a foreign land and turned into a virtual sex slave. She was one of the lucky ones—she had escaped to South Korea. But it was clear that many others are still in captivity in China, still helpless, with no one to turn to.

The only glimmer of hope for many of these women is

that they have access to the Internet, which means they can find information about the underground railroad. Even that is not easy—the Chinese government censors some Internet sites, so to find the information they need, these women may have to get through censors' blocks. Kay told us that she managed to get in touch with Pastor Chun, who used his contacts to help arrange her escape from China and ultimately make it to South Korea. The plan was for her to join a group of other North Koreans who were also trying to make that last leap to freedom: They would attempt to escape China by train.

On the appointed day, the group boarded a train with fake Chinese IDs. Kay nervously took her seat, and like the other defectors, she spoke as little as possible to avoid revealing that she wasn't Chinese. During the night, as she lay in her cramped bunk, she heard officers coming through and checking IDs. She pulled her blanket up over her head and prayed that the officers would just keep going. To her relief, they did.

Unlike the twelve North Koreans in *Seoul Train* who were captured at the Mongolian border, this group made it to safety. Once Kay had successfully escaped China, she was able to travel freely to South Korea, where she intended to stay.

The stories of defectors who made it to South Korea were inspiring and uplifting, but they were also filled with sadness. Kay was happy to be free—but it meant she might never see her family again, an idea that sent chills through me. These were some of the most wrenching moments in our interviews—the moments when defectors spoke of those loved ones they had left behind.

After lunch, we interviewed the same two men we'd spoken with the day before. One showed us a photo of his father, dressed in the uniform of the North Korean army. He'd learned that his father had passed away, and as I looked at the photo, I saw how much the father and the son looked alike. This was the legacy of the Korean war and the decades that followed: parents and children, brothers and sisters, separated. The same blood ran in their veins, but they were forever kept apart by the vagaries of war and ideology.

Later that afternoon, Laura, Mitch, and I spoke with two South Korean newspaper reporters who had covered the issue of defectors, too. We asked for their advice about gathering information in China, where they had spent ten months reporting. They were very helpful, giving us advice on whom we could approach for interviews and even whom we could trust. "There are double agents," one of them said, warning us that we needed to be extremely careful about whom we dealt with. Their warnings gave me pause, but we were deep into the project now, so we had no real choice but to plunge ahead and believe the contacts we had would be trustworthy.

When I had been in touch with one of these reporters before leaving L.A., he had recommended someone who could serve as our guide while in China. I had asked Pastor Chun about the man, and he had already arranged for him to be our guide. Because this man did so much work with the underground railroad, he was apparently quite secretive, but the reporter assured us that if Pastor Chun recommended him, we could trust him. This was the guide who would, one week later, take us to the Tumen River.

We interviewed Pastor Chun that afternoon, and he told us more about the North Korean women who are forced into Internet sex work. He even opened up an MSN chat window with two of them and asked if we could interview them when we were in China. He also set us up to meet a man who ran foster homes in China for North Korean children. We would contact all these people through Pastor Chun.

Just before we left Pastor Chun, he asked if we had a cell phone. We said no, and he said, "It would be good to have one for China." We'd be on the road much of the time there, traveling to different venues to shoot footage and do interviews, so it would be much easier to communicate with contacts if we had a cell phone.

Pastor Chun turned and yanked open a drawer in his desk, and I saw dozens of cell phones piled inside. "Here," he said, grabbing one and handing it to me, "use this, and just return it when you get back." Armed with the cell phone and the guide's number, we felt at least a little more prepared. Pastor Chun led us all in prayer, and we left his office at about 5 in the evening. We would leave for China the next morning.

Back at our hotel, Laura, Mitch, and I all had dinner at the restaurant. We joked around about enjoying our meal now because the food in China would be a whole different story, and we talked about what we might face while we were there. We were excited, but also aware of the huge amount of work that lay ahead of us.

Toward the end of dinner, my mother came to the hotel so we could spend some time together before the next phase of my trip. Mom had brought me a hat and coat to wear, knowing it would be cold up in the northeastern part of China. She stayed over in my hotel room, and we talked long into the night about my work, about Hana and Michael, about my life in America. Like many mothers and daughters, my mom and I have sometimes had a complicated relationship, but that night I think she was proud of me.

The next morning, I woke up full of energy. My conversations with my mom had left me feeling so positive about the work ahead of me in China. We had breakfast together at the hotel restaurant, sitting near a window that overlooked Seoul. We joked about how relaxing it was to linger over coffee as we watched the city come to life below us. She asked me to help with a project at her church when I returned the next week. I felt so connected to her and so happy in her company. As she left the hotel, I was already looking forward to seeing her again. "I'll see you next week, Mom," I said. She waved as she rode off in a taxi.

With that, I turned my attention to the next leg of our journey. Everything had gone really well so far, and I hoped the same would be true in China.

Three

A FOOT ON EACH SIDE

O<small>N</small> F<small>RIDAY</small>, M<small>ARCH</small> 13, Laura, Mitch, and I flew from Seoul to Yanji, a city in the far northeast of China. Just under twenty miles from North Korea, Yanji was the perfect place to seek out defectors and get footage of the Tumen River flowing between the two countries. The work we'd do this coming week would make or break our documentary, and we were eager to get started.

After meeting the North Korean defectors in Seoul, I felt much more personally connected to the story we were trying to tell. It was one thing to do research about defectors while back in L.A., but another thing entirely to meet and talk with them. And arriving in this part of China, I realized that any-one could be a defector. At the passport-control station in the airport, I watched as Chinese officers pulled aside a man in shabby clothes, presumably for questioning. Was he a defector? What was his story?

As we rode away from the airport in a taxi, I could see that many signs, including street signs, were written in both Chinese and Korean. Yanji is the capital of China's Yanbian Korean Autonomous Prefecture, a region where over 40 percent of the residents are ethnic Koreans. It's like another Asian country—not China and not Korea, but something in between.

Because there are so many Koreans here, China has designated Korean a second "official" language in the prefecture. This helps the North Korean defectors who flee across the Tumen River into this region—but only to a degree. They blend in more easily here than in other parts of China, but they're still at constant risk of being sent back by Chinese authorities. They might look like Chinese citizens, but because they don't speak Chinese, they stand a good chance of being caught.

Pastor Chun had given me two phone numbers—one for the guide, and one for a man named Mr. Lee who ran the foster homes for North Korean children. I called them both when we arrived at the hotel and set up meetings for that evening.

Mr. Lee came first, at about 6:30 P.M. His clothes were clean and pressed, and he spoke some English in addition to impeccable Korean. He was obviously very educated, but he also had a warmth and humility about him. We sat down in the hotel's restaurant to have dinner, and he told us about the work he was doing.

He ran several foster homes in the area, homes for children of North Korean mothers and Chinese fathers. In most cases, the children's mothers had been lured to China much as the bookkeeper we interviewed in Seoul was—with promises of legitimate work and a chance to send money back home. But once they arrived, they were forced into marriages with Chinese men, as the people they thought would help them ended up trafficking them into a kind of marriage slavery.

The women forced into these arranged marriages are in an impossible situation. They can't go to the authorities, or they will be arrested and sent back to North Korea. If they leave their new "husbands," they have nowhere to go and no way to earn money. Often, the men who pay for North Korean wives are farmers in remote areas, so the women are completely isolated from the rest of the world. The prospects for escaping safely, without ending up in prison back in North Korea, are bleak.

The children produced in these marriages are at a big disadvantage, too. Because their fathers are Chinese, they can technically receive Chinese citizenship—but to do so, the family must report who the mother is, too. Their mothers are illegal immigrants, though, so reporting their identities could put them in danger. These children are being raised in homes where their mothers are essentially held against their will. And when a North Korean mother either can't take it anymore and flees, or is discovered, arrested, and sent back to North Korea, the children are left with a father who in many cases is unable to care for them.

This is where Mr. Lee steps in. He places such children in secret homes, where they'll be looked after by women or couples who've been enlisted in the cause. By making sure the children are well fed, educated, and sheltered, Mr. Lee is helping to save them from a life on the streets.

Our dinner closed with Mr. Lee agreeing to let us meet some of the children in the next day or two. But Mr. Lee didn't leave just yet. He knew our guide was coming to the hotel at 8 P.M., and he made it clear he didn't want to cross paths with him. Even though they were both working for the same cause, he—like many who worked with the underground railroad—tried to stay as low-profile as possible. So I went to meet the guide in the lobby and took him up to my room, while Mr. Lee stayed in the restaurant. After a few minutes had passed, Mr. Lee left and Mitch and Laura came up, too.

The guide looked very different from Mr. Lee. He wore dark clothes and had a tendency to glance around nervously. He sat hunched over and had a look of distrust on his face, and he seemed uncomfortable in our presence. We knew almost nothing about him, having heard only that he had experience with North Korean defectors as well as international media, and that he had recently been in some kind of trouble with the authorities. But he didn't tell us anything about himself, instead just listening as we told him the kinds of people we wanted to interview and the places we wanted to film. We explained that we had only a week in China so our time was limited. Could he help us arrange all the things we needed to do?

"I have to look into it," he said. We asked him several more specific questions to figure out if he could get us what we needed, but each time he gave equally vague answers. He refused to make any promises, but just told us to meet him in the lobby the next morning at 10. And with that, he left.

I went to sleep that night with my head swimming. Would the guide be able to make the arrangements we needed? Would we have time to shoot enough material to really show the hardships these defectors were facing?

We had gotten great footage in Seoul, and I was hoping to build on that momentum in China. But our guide was frustratingly vague about everything. Privately, I questioned whether he would really come through for us, but I didn't want Laura and Mitch to know how worried I was. Because I had done the research and set up the trip, I felt responsible for the situation we were in. I was determined to find a way to succeed even if our guide was unreliable.

The next morning, the guide got to our hotel late, which didn't help matters. Mitch, Laura, and I were waiting in the lobby, eager to get a jump on the day and already stressed about time. But when we got going, we started getting good footage almost immediately.

We went to a market that looked like a giant cell phone convention, with rows of booths selling phones and accessories. I shot Laura doing a standup about the booming cell phone business in China and how it was helping people to communicate with relatives in North Korea. I bought a Chinese SIM card for the cell phone Pastor Chun had given me, and Mitch shot some B-roll footage. Afterward, we went to our next stop: the Tumen Bridge, which stretches across the Tumen River between China and North Korea.

Although the border between the two countries is patrolled, tourists are allowed to walk out to the middle of this bridge to put one foot in North Korean territory and one foot in Chinese. Mitch, Laura, and I walked to the middle, pretending to be tourists while trying to secretly shoot some footage. We each put one foot into North Korean territory, then spent a few minutes looking the rest of the way across the river. It felt strange that North Korea was just across the bridge, an easy walk away. The land I had heard so many horror stories about looked quiet and not much different from the Chinese side.

We walked back across the bridge to China. Along the riverbank, small shops sold North Korean currency as souvenirs, along with cigarettes, sodas, and snacks. We looked at the various North Korean bills—colorful banknotes with heroic portraits of Kim Il-sung, soldiers, factory workers, and countryside scenes—and Laura even bought some to take home for colleagues. We also went into a riverfront building that had a telescope for public viewing. Looking through the telescope at North Koreans pushing carts on the other shore, I marveled once again at how close the two countries really are.

Next, the guide took us to another, more remote area farther down the river. He pointed out a closed-circuit camera near the riverbank; it was pointed toward the North Korean side.

"One year, about eight kids crossed the river, running on the ice," he said. "North Korean soldiers shot and killed them. After that, the Chinese put this camera up." It was a sobering reminder that, as at the Berlin Wall during the Cold War years, soldiers along the border will shoot to kill if they see people trying to escape. No one knows the exact number, but in the nearly six decades since the Korean War ended, it's safe to assume that hundreds, if not thousands, of people have been killed in this way.

Because of this tense history—complete with spies, hidden cameras, desperate refugees, and armed soldiers—the river has an eerie atmosphere. As we walked toward the edge of the riverbank, I was already feeling on high alert. And when I suddenly noticed two men standing nearby, dressed in identical dark blue coats and dark hats, it freaked me out. I turned quickly, trying to hide my camera, as I feared we could get in trouble with Chinese authorities for shooting footage at the river. Mitch, too, was spooked by their presence, and he also turned away from them quickly.

As we started back toward the taxi, Laura was the only one who didn't appear rattled. "Walk slowly," she said quietly. "Be calm." Then she turned to the men and greeted them with a bright "Hi!" They didn't reply, so we just kept heading back up toward our car. The two men could have been anyone—Chinese agents, a couple of guys doing business, or maybe even just friends on their lunch break. We'd never know. But their mere presence had made us jumpy, reminding me that we needed at all times to be aware of who was watching.

And we weren't the only ones who were apprehensive. Pastor Chun had arranged for us to interview a North Korean defector who was being forced to work in the Internet sex trade, but when she called my cell phone, the first thing she told me was that she was scared. It was definitely risky for her to talk with us—if her "employers" found out, she could get beaten or worse.

I wanted to persuade her, but knowing the fear and shame she must have felt, and the risk involved, I couldn't push her. I desperately wanted to tell her story, but I also didn't want to be the kind of journalist who cares more about the story than about someone's life. We talked for ten minutes or so, but in the end she was too frightened to meet with us.

The rest of that day, Laura, Mitch, and I rode around shooting B-roll in various locations. By the time we got back to the hotel, I felt frustrated. We had lots of fill-in footage, but we needed to get interviews to really tell the story. I hoped the next day would prove to be more fruitful.

❁

The next morning, Sunday, March 15, we got a late start. We also had a long drive ahead of us to our next appointment, so the day started off a bit tense.

We drove about four hours out of Yanji, deeper into the countryside and farther away from North Korea. Along the way, our car was waved down at a police checkpoint and an officer asked for my passport information. Fortunately, he didn't seem all that curious as to why Mitch, Laura, and I might be poking around in rural China, so he let us go. We continued on, as the houses by the roadside became smaller and more run-down, evidence of how poverty-stricken these rural areas are.

The guide had arranged for us to meet a North Korean woman who was married to a poor Chinese farmer. She was nervous but had bravely agreed to let us interview her. We met her at a neutral location so we wouldn't have any details of where she lived, and she told us her story.

She had crossed the Tumen River about four years earlier in hopes of making money in China to bring home. She never planned to stay permanently, as she had a family, including three children, in North Korea. But once she got to China, she realized she had no way of supporting herself, since she had no legal paperwork and couldn't risk getting caught by working illegally. There was only one option that would allow her to live in relative security and still bring in some money: A relative in China sold her to a farmer who couldn't find a wife on his own.

The woman wasn't abused, and the farmer fed and sheltered her. But she hadn't been able to see her children in North Korea in four long years, and had spoken with them on the phone only once. She asked them if they wanted to come live with her in China, and they said no. She still wanted to return to North Korea, but it wasn't clear when she would be able to go. Once, she had actually made her way to the banks of the Tumen River in an attempt to cross back to North Korea, but recent rains had swollen the river so much that she feared she would drown before making it across. So far, she hadn't tried again.

The interesting thing was that this woman had no real opinion about politics or government. She had nothing bad to say about the regime in North Korea. She simply had wanted to earn enough money to have a better life, and that's what had brought her to China. But home was, and always would be, North Korea.

Before leaving, I gave the woman 500 yuan. It wasn't a lot of money by U.S. standards—only about $75—but it was more than she earned in a month. She smiled gratefully. We thanked her for talking with us and piled back into the car.

We had to get back to Yanji, because Mr. Lee had invited us to come for dinner at one of the foster homes that evening. As we drove back, I thought about the woman and what she'd told us. I could feel her pain when she talked about her children and sensed she had lost all hope of seeing them again. The idea of being separated from my child for years on end, with no idea when—or even if—I would ever see her again was too painful to contemplate. I tried to console myself with the fact that, even if the children didn't have their mother, at least the three of them had each other.

We dropped off the guide before going to pick up Mr. Lee at his apartment, as he wanted as few people as possible to know where he lived. On the way, we stopped at a market to buy some food and gifts for the children. I was looking forward to seeing them, and I hoped they would be comfortable with us and eventually with our cameras. As it turned out, they were—apparently, we were not the first camera crew to visit the foster home.

The kids seemed very happy that we were visiting them. They all seemed well taken care of, with bright faces and clean clothes. And I was happy to be visiting with them, too—they were so eager and inquisitive! It felt like a breath of fresh air, amid the hardship and pain we'd already witnessed, to see these children being cared for so well.

Despite their circumstances, they acted just like any other kids. They wanted to tell me all about what they knew, to show off how well they could dance, sing, and read. These children reminded me so much of Hana, who always wants me to notice and praise her for her skills. Watching them, and telling them how well they did things, made me realize all over again how much we adults can make a difference in the lives of children just by paying attention and giving them simple praise.

At our first meeting, I had asked Mr. Lee if we could film the children, and I told him we would make sure their identities were protected. He'd said we could, but now, as I was shooting B-roll, the kids were jumping around so much that it was impossible to make sure no faces got filmed. I told Mr. Lee we would digitally blur their faces later, and he nodded and smiled. I assumed this meant he was okay with our continuing to film.

One girl in particular attached herself to me and wouldn't leave my side. She looked and acted as if she was about six years old, but when I asked, I was told she was nine. I asked Mr. Lee if I could interview her. He said yes and offered a quiet side room where we could talk. I walked with the girl into the room and started asking her a few questions.

I started off with how she had come to the foster home and what life was like there. At first, I didn't want to ask about her mother, thinking it might be too painful for her, but as we talked the conversation naturally went toward her family. She told me she missed her dad and brothers, but said that her dad was happy she was studying hard. She said her mother had run away and that she missed her, too. Oddly, it seemed as if I was more sensitive about her mother's absence than the girl was—she spoke of her mother easily, without seeming at all upset.

At this point, the girl took my hand and looked into my

eyes. "Can you visit me again?" she asked. And I burst into tears. It was so wrenching, the thought of this little girl without her mother, and hearing her ask so plaintively if I could come back was too much. Surprised by my tears, she pulled her hand away. But I took her hand again in mine. I wanted so badly to comfort her, but I also didn't want to tell her anything that wasn't true.

"I don't know if I can promise you that," I said, "but I'll write a letter to you." She nodded and said, "Okay." As I had at the church service in Seoul, I felt overwhelmed by the emotions I was experiencing. I was supposed to be an objective journalist covering a story, but at that moment I responded as anyone would, with deep feelings of sorrow and empathy for this girl and for all the other girls and boys like her. It took me a few moments to compose myself.

We had dinner with the children and shot some more footage around the foster home. And as the evening wound down, Mr. Lee and I talked about the kind of help he needed to keep these homes going. I told him I would try to raise awareness of his work through my church back in Los Angeles, and Laura gave him 1,000 yuan—about $150. He asked that we send any other help we could through Pastor Chun.

I was impressed by the work Mr. Lee was doing, and I was happy to play a small part in letting people know about it. We thanked him, hugged the children good-bye, and headed back to the hotel. My head was full of images from the day, and I knew tomorrow would be just as full.

❈

Monday, March 16, started off well. We were happy about the footage we'd gotten the day before and we had interviews set up for the day. Our first one was with a woman who was being forced to work in the Internet sex trade. We took a taxi without the guide, to protect her identity, and brought her to a nearby hotel for the interview.

This was the same woman we had first seen via the MSN chat room while in Pastor Chun's office. Unlike the woman I'd spoken to by phone the day before, who was too frightened to meet with us, this woman, whom I'll call Young, seemed very open and relaxed. She even seemed relatively comfortable with the line of work she'd been forced into. "I met a really nice guy who takes care of me," she told us. But still, her life was rigidly controlled by the men who made money off her.

"I'm allowed to go outside every once in a while," she said, explaining how she was able to meet with us. "I just have to report it."

Young had left North Korea after having a fight with her mother. But when she arrived in China, the welcome was harsh: The men who met her at the border took her to a small room and handcuffed her to a heater, and her guard, who spoke no Korean, sometimes beat her. Her captors told her that she had to bring in a minimum of 300,000 Korean won a day—around $250—or she wouldn't earn anything herself.

This meant she would have to work hours on end, engaging in sex talk and undressing on camera for strangers, to get paid anything at all.

Her captors also told her they were putting money aside for her, money that they'd give her at some unspecified future time. Young apparently believed this, although it was almost certainly not true—yet perhaps this optimism was what allowed her to work in such conditions without despair. She also had big dreams of making it to Seoul and living like the people on her favorite South Korean TV show, which she watched online. It was a kind of soap opera, a show about rich people living the high life—a life that was almost certainly out of this girl's reach. But this was her dream, and it sustained her. In fact, she believed in it so fully that her whole attitude was bright and cheery despite her situation.

During the interview, we seemed far more nervous for Young than she was for herself. I asked her if she needed to get back before her guards got upset, and she said no, that we could even go and have lunch together. So we took her out and bought her lunch, and at the end, I pressed 2,000 yuan—about $300—into her hand, which was the amount Pastor Chun had suggested when he arranged the interview. It wasn't enough for her to pay an escape broker to get out of China—that would cost about 10,000 yuan. But it was a start.

"Hide this," I told her. "Don't tell anyone you have it. Use it for when you escape." She said she would.

As Mitch, Laura, and I rode away in the taxi, I couldn't help but think about the people we'd met so far and their desperate struggles not only to survive, but to survive with dignity. They seemed to wear their hardships in their expressions—I could sense a kind of darkness even when they smiled. It was sobering to realize that risking their lives physically to escape North Korea was only the beginning of their struggles, all in the name of finding freedom and basic human rights. Yet it also struck me that humans are strong and can adapt to the environment they find themselves in. That's what these defectors had done, because it was what they had to do to survive.

We picked up the guide, who had arranged a meeting for us with a young man who had very recently escaped from North Korea. We drove for about an hour, intending to meet him, like the farmer's wife, in a neutral place in order to keep where he lived a secret.

On the way, the guide's phone rang. He answered it, had a very short conversation, and hung up. "That was a North Korean officer," he said casually.

"Really?" I asked, amazed. I knew he had contacts with border guards, but I didn't expect that he'd actually get calls on his cell phone from them. "How do you know an officer in North Korea?"

"He often calls me," the guide answered. I made a mental note to ask if we could film a phone conversation with the North Korean officer, thinking it would make a good addition to the documentary.

When we arrived at our destination, we were met by a

pastor who had worked with our guide to set up the meet-ing. We exchanged greetings, and he asked me, "Why are you here wandering around China? Why do you want to do this dangerous work?" I explained that we were hoping to spread the word about the defectors' situation. "God bless you," he replied—a blessing I needed that day, and gladly accepted.

The pastor introduced us to the young defector, a for-mer North Korean army officer, but the man apparently hadn't been told we were planning to interview him. He was scared—afraid that speaking publicly might somehow put him in danger. I understood his fear, but I tried to explain how his participation could help others. I told him we worked for Current TV, a small network that covered stories other peo-ple wouldn't talk about. "Your appearance could help thou-sands of others in the same situation," I said.

His hesitation spoke volumes about the degree of fear he felt, so I did something I had never done before. With my camera at my side, I pushed the record button before he had agreed to it. The camera was pointed down, so there was no visual of him, but it captured audio as we spoke for a few more minutes. The fear in his voice was a powerful sign of how frightening the situation was for defectors like him.

At one point while the audio was recording, I told him I was a Christian and explained that I felt in some ways that telling this story was God's calling for me. When he agreed to do the interview a few moments later, I was relieved. I didn't know if we would ever use that first bit of tape or not, since now we would have an actual interview. But later, that brief clip would become relevant to my own situation in a way I never would have guessed.

Unlike the other defectors we had interviewed so far, this man was highly educated and had very strong opinions about the political situation in North Korea—in fact, it was the political situation that had compelled him to flee. He had served in the army for many years, but little by little he began to understand that the propaganda he was hearing was all lies. North Korea was in theory a socialist country, but those were only slogans, he said. In truth, those in power were corrupted, even more so than in capitalist countries. Higher-ranking government officials routinely hoarded food and money, keeping ordinary North Koreans ill-fed and poor.

His was the story of the real disillusionment inside North Korea—the story that no one we had interviewed so far had articulated. Even though he was talking about the problems of the country he had chosen to leave, I sensed he still cared for his motherland, and his internal conflict was deeply moving. I could feel his hurt and bitterness, as well as his nervousness in expressing it, and I had real sympathy for him.

Part of the reason he was nervous was that this was his second time fleeing from North Korea. The previous time, he told us, he'd been captured and sent to a labor camp. I asked how he escaped the camp, and he said he couldn't even imagine how he'd done it. Maybe he simply didn't want to give any details, or maybe he really didn't remember. What was clear was that he couldn't quite believe he had actually managed to escape—and that he had no intention of getting caught and sent back again.

He also talked about one of the uncomfortable truths for the people who flee North Korea: that by defecting they put the families they leave behind in very difficult situations. When the North Korean government finds out that someone has defected, the family members immediately come under suspicion. What did they know? Did they help out in any way? Those left behind are subject to interrogations and punishment, even if they had no idea the person was planning to defect. And, of course, if they really did have no idea, that's incredibly painful in and of itself.

He acknowledged that by fleeing he put his own family in danger, but said that he was unable to live anymore under the shadow of the North Korean regime. In fact, he said he believed that his leaving would change his children's life for the better, but I never was able to find out what he meant by that. Was he planning to bring his children out of North Korea, too? It wasn't clear.

The more the man spoke with us, the more nervous he became. "We'll talk later," he said, then asked if there was any way we could help him. He needed money to pay a broker to get him out of China, but money was hard to come by. Until he could somehow get the sum he needed, he was stuck living deep underground, in an extremely rural area with no Internet connection, no phone, nothing to help him get it.

I really wanted to help this man, whom I felt a connection with, so I offered him 500 yuan out of my own pocket. But he refused it, apparently too embarrassed to accept my personal money. I told him that once we got back to Seoul I'd ask Pastor Chun if he could help. This felt like a really inadequate response to the problems he faced, but it was all I had to offer.

I left the interview and rejoined our guide. He saw the look on my face and asked if I felt bad for the defectors. "I'm worried for them," I said.

But the guide responded bitterly, scoffing that "Another network's interpreter held the refugees and cried after the interviews." What was he saying? That I would forget about the refugees? That all I cared about was making the documentary? He may have thought that, but he was wrong.

Back in the car, I found myself getting depressed. So many people were suffering—living under the constant threat of arrest or being held against their will. Why should this defector, who seemed like an honest, decent, kind person, be forced to hide in the countryside in fear? How could we ever hope to help the thousands of people whose lives had been upended? Thousands of miles away from my own family, running from morning to night to document the pain these people were experiencing, I began to feel smothered by the stress.

And I wasn't the only one feeling it. When we stopped at a nearby tea house to plan our next move, Mitch, Laura, and I were all tired and upset, and we began bickering about what we should shoot next. We didn't have anything set up for the evening, and with time so short, I was afraid to waste even a minute.

"How about if we go to the Tumen River to shoot tonight?" I asked. "We could just wait there, describe how cold and isolated it is, and maybe if we're lucky we'll see someone." I knew the chances of actually seeing someone crossing the river were slim. But I wanted us to experience what it felt like for defectors, hiding at the border in the cold and dark, fearing that someone might see them. If we experienced even a fraction of what they felt, we could describe it much better in the documentary.

But Mitch disagreed, not wanting to make the trek back to the river at night. We argued back and forth, with Laura trying to find some middle ground. The guide, who was with us, knew we were arguing—but he didn't know what we were saying since he spoke no English.

For the first time, I felt disappointed. This was a difficult, scary story, and we needed to push as deeply into it as possible. How could we bring attention to the plight of the refugees if we had only interviews, with no footage to illustrate what they actually went through? We were already at a disadvantage, because we had so little time to spend with the people we were interviewing—we just came in, spoke with them for a couple of hours, and left. To really tell the story properly, we'd need to spend days, not hours, with our subjects. But, of course, we didn't have nearly enough time for that.

At some point, the guide said that he could walk out to

the middle of the river and we could shoot some footage of him there. This would be powerful footage, but it didn't seem right to me—this wasn't the guide's responsibility, and it seemed wrong to put him in a dangerous situation to get the footage we needed.

"No," I told him. "If anything happens to you, I couldn't forgive myself."

"I'm okay," he said. "He is with me." I'm not sure if the guide was Christian, but it was clear that he was putting his faith in his God, and his simple statement stopped me cold. I suddenly realized that I hadn't been very faithful to my God, whom I'd all but forgotten in the course of chasing this story. I decided I would put my faith in Him now, and when the guide suggested another idea—that he and I should walk to the middle of the river—I immediately said, "I'll do it."

Mitch was definitely not in favor of this plan, and he and I went back and forth, debating whether it was a good idea, until Laura finally spoke up. "I'll go, too," she said.

This was apparently enough to convince Mitch that the team should stick together. "Okay," he said. "We'll go tomorrow morning, first thing." So, instead of driving back to Yanji, we decided to find a place to sleep nearby so we could get up early and go to the river the next day. I bought some necessities—a toothbrush, and some bread and chocolate to carry with us the next day—and we found a modest hotel where we could get a few hours' sleep. Tomorrow would be our last day in Yanji, and if we could get the footage at the river and record a phone call with the North Korean officer, I would feel satis-fied that we'd done all we could. Our to-do list was almost all checked off, and the only other task we had in China was to shoot some extra material as B-roll.

The guide had arranged to call the North Korean officer at 10:30 P.M., so Mitch and I made sure we were ready with our cameras to film the conversation. But when he dialed the officer's number, no one answered.

"I think I'm a few minutes late," he said. Disappointed, Mitch and Laura called it a night. We were planning to meet at 3:40 A.M. the next day, so they decided to get some sleep. But I wasn't quite ready to quit for the night. I had planned for two more scenes, and one—the phone call with the offi-cer—was now gone. I needed to replace it with something else, so I decided to take the guide to get something to eat and talk to him a little more about his experiences and his work, to see if I could get any other ideas.

Up to this point, the guide had said very little about him-self, but as we talked, he started to open up. A few months earlier, one of his contacts in North Korea had asked him to come across the border—but it had been a trap. He was cap-tured and beaten, but he managed to escape. He wouldn't tell me how he escaped, though, just saying that "When one makes promises, one must keep them"—a phrase he repeated several times.

The way he kept emphasizing this statement seemed odd to me. It was as if he believed that keeping a promise—any promise—was a life-or-death matter, trumping every other consideration. It seemed silly, almost naïve, to cling to such a belief, and I wondered why it was so important to him.

Later, after Laura and I were captured, I would spend hours wondering what the guide really meant. Had he promised something to the North Koreans in return for being allowed to escape? Had he offered to bring them someone else—possibly Laura, Mitch, and me? The more I thought about it, the more I wondered. What else could explain the low hooting noise the guide made as we crossed the river that fateful morning of March 17? Did he betray us?

But these questions were all in the future. At that point, I trusted the guide completely—so completely, in fact, that I asked him to take me to the river that night. I didn't know what the situation would be in the morning, or how much time we'd have to shoot, so I wanted to get some footage while I could.

I felt driven to get as much material as possible, partly because it seemed as if Laura and Mitch were unhappy with the guide. He hadn't set up very many interviews—most of our contacts had come from Pastor Chun—even though we were paying him decent money. As the only Korean speaker on our team, I expected myself to be able to get more from the guide. What else besides interviews could he help us with? How could I maximize the use of his time? That evening, even though it was late, I knew there was one thing he could do for us.

"Can you take me to the border now?" I asked the guide, as the clock ticked toward 11 P.M. He said yes.

❈

The guide drove me to a spot just a short walk away from the riverbank. As we got out of the car, I asked, "Can I follow you from behind with the camera? I'll only shoot from your legs down." I wanted to get footage of an anonymous person at the riverbank, to dramatize the role of the brokers who dealt in human cargo.

"People will recognize my shoes," the guide said, unwilling to take the slightest chance of revealing himself on camera.

"Then let's switch," I suggested. "You can wear mine. I bought them ten years ago—no one will know it's you." We swapped shoes and set out for the river, climbing over a low brick wall and walking toward the brush and trees that lined the bank.

It was pitch black, with the moon casting only the faintest glow. Across the river, the North Korean side was invisible in the blackness. In the still of the night, I could hear running water—the ice on the river was melting.

He walked toward the riverbank and I followed, filming him with night vision, which showed his legs as a ghostly apparition moving through the bushes. As we walked, I couldn't make out anything except what was right in front of me. Suddenly, as we neared the river, I got a very strange feeling. I stopped dead in my tracks and said, "We should go back. I can't see anything."

The guide turned around and we headed back toward the bushes we'd just come through. Just then, I heard a strange sound. It was metal grinding against metal, coming from somewhere across the river.

"What is that?" I asked.

"I don't know," he said. "I've never heard it before." It sounded like trucks, but it was hard to tell for sure.

"Let's go back," I said, feeling nervous. Suddenly, all I wanted was to get away from the river and back across that brick wall. The guide began walking very fast, and I followed him through the blackness.

At that moment, I heard a sound. It seemed like a female voice, but I couldn't tell anything more. A chill shot down my back, and all I could think was, *Keep moving!* I didn't look right or left, but just kept plowing straight ahead, trying to get to the car as quickly as possible.

Once we made it back to the car, the guide and I switched our shoes back and returned to the hotel. Relieved to be back safely, I showed him the footage so he could confirm there was no way to identify him from what I'd shot. "It looks good, huh?" he said, seeming pleased. We said goodnight and I headed up to my room. By now it was 1 A.M., and we were planning to leave for the river at 3:40, so I had very little time to sleep. I laid my head on the pillow—and just then the cell phone rang.

It was Pastor Chun. "How's everything going?" he asked.

"Very well," I told him. "We're going to the border first thing in the morning to shoot some footage there."

"Be careful," he said. "Do you need to meet with any more sex workers?"

"I don't think so," I replied. "We don't have enough time."

"Okay," he said. Then once again he said, "Be careful." It was the last time I would talk to him.

I finally fell asleep, and the next thing I knew, my phone was ringing again. Groggily, I answered it.

"Euna! I've been pounding on your door!" It was Laura, sounding agitated. "I called to you so many times, I thought you were dead!" I looked at my watch: It was past 4 A.M. Where was the guide? He was supposed to wake us! "Come on!" said Laura. "We've got to go!"

I called the guide on his cell phone and told him to come to the lobby, then grabbed my backpack and camera and hurried down myself. "I'm sorry I overslept!" I told Mitch and Laura. "The guide and I went to the river last night, and I got to sleep late." They were surprised, but we didn't discuss it— we just jumped into the car to make up for lost time.

We needed to get to the river and shoot before the sun came up so the Chinese authorities wouldn't see us. Mentally and physically exhausted, but fueled by adrenaline, we made our way to the river in the predawn darkness. The guide took us to a different spot than where we'd been the night before—a more remote area where we were unlikely to be spotted even as the sun came up.

I hoped we could get our footage quickly and get back to town to shoot a market we had skipped the day before. And just maybe, if we got everything done, I'd even be able to grab an hour or two of sleep. But as it turned out, many hours would pass before I would sleep again. And when I did, it would be in a jail cell in North Korea.

Four

PRISONER'S DILEMMA

EVERYTHING HAPPENED SO FAST that morning at the Tumen River that it was hard to take it all in. One moment, Laura and I were free citizens, journalists doing the job we'd come to China to do. And the next, we were prisoners, bruised and battered—and scared.

From the time we stepped onto the ice to the time the soldiers dragged us into North Korean territory, not even an hour had passed. Nothing that was happening seemed real. Were we really being held prisoner by armed guards? Where were they taking us? I looked at Laura and saw that her head was still bleeding. How had this all happened? And what would happen now?

The soldiers marched us deeper into North Korean territory, with one guarding us and the other carrying my backpack and Laura's tote bag. I was so cold, my teeth were chattering—my pants were wet from being dragged on the ice, and I had left my coat in the middle of the river so the North Koreans wouldn't find the phone numbers in my pocket. In an effort to keep warm, I stuffed my hands into my pants pockets—and realized with horror that I still had the cell phone Pastor Chun had given me, as well as a small videotape cassette.

I wasn't sure exactly what was on the tape, but there was probably footage from interviews we'd done. And the cell phone had a record of the numbers we'd called to set those interviews up. I had to get rid of them somehow—lives could be in danger if the North Koreans got their hands on either the phone or the tape. As the soldiers marched along beside us, I waited for a moment when they were talking to each other and not paying close attention to us. I pretended to stumble as I dropped the phone and tape down the riverbank. To my relief, the soldiers didn't notice.

The soldiers marched us about a half-mile or so to a tunnel. We went through it, then up a hill on the other side, before arriving at a small military base. Though the base—a couple of small buildings and an exercise yard—was pretty close to the river, we hadn't seen any sign of it from the other side, as it was completely hidden by trees and thick brush.

We were led to a gray, one-story, matchbox-shaped building, and one soldier stayed with us while the other went inside to report our capture. There was a patch of dirt nearby that apparently served as the exercise yard, but no one was in it. Even so, as soon as we arrived, ten to fifteen soldiers suddenly appeared and crowded around us. They stared at us in wonder, as if they'd never seen women who looked like us before.

The strange thing was, I had never seen men like them before. They were all very short, most of them only slightly taller than me and very slender. They were soldiers, but they were built like boys. I knew from my research that, because of the years of famine and poor nutrition, North Koreans are on average much shorter than their counterparts in richer countries: The average North Korean man is under five feet, five inches tall, while the average American man is about five-ten. But reading about this was one thing—seeing the difference in the soldiers crowding around me was another.

The soldiers were murmuring among themselves, and it was hard for me to hear what they were saying. One asked me in Korean, "How old are you?" When I told him I was thirty-six, he laughed and said, "You're not thirty-six!" He shook his head in disbelief, then said, "Who are you?"

"Students," I replied. I had thought about what we should say if we got into any trouble with Chinese authorities, even joking about it with Mitch on our flight to Seoul. But now the joke had become serious, and it seemed like this would be our best cover. If the North Koreans believed we were really students, just following the instructions of our "professor," they might let us go. But if they realized we were doing a story for the media about North Korean defectors, they would no doubt be angry—and who knows what would happen to us then?

But my answer just seemed to confuse the soldier. Perhaps he didn't believe a thirty-six-year-old could be a student, or that I was thirty-six at all. "You are a student?" he repeated. Then he said something I didn't understand. I stared at him, and he said it again. It wasn't until the fourth or fifth time he said it that I realized he was trying to speak English to me. Even though we had just been speaking Korean to each other, he somehow understood that I was from somewhere else. He was saying, "Democratic People's Republic of Korea," over and over, but his accent was so thick it was almost incomprehensible.

An officer came out and ordered the soldiers to return to their positions, and all of them shuffled away except for the one who was guarding us. Suddenly, Laura turned to me. "Where's your coat?" she asked, a look of concern on her face.

"I left it at the river," I whispered. "There were phone numbers in my pocket." She moved closer and put her arm around me, rubbing my shoulders in an effort to stop my shivering. "Laura," I said, "will you pray with me?" I didn't know what was in store for us, but I knew we needed His protection. "Lord, please give us your peace and watch over us," I intoned quietly. "Please give the North Koreans compassion and have them be generous to us. Amen."

"Stop talking," the soldier watching us said, eyeing us warily.

"But she doesn't speak Korean," I told him. "I need to translate things for her. She can't understand what's going on." This was true—Laura couldn't understand a word of what anyone was saying, which only made the situation more frightening for her. She had a look of shock and fear on her face, her hair was matted with blood, and her whole body was shaking. I had never seen her look so weak and lost, and I was worried about her.

I wanted to translate for Laura, but there was another reason I wanted to be able to speak English—so we could talk without getting into trouble. The soldiers didn't understand English, which meant we could plan our strategy for how to deal with this confusing, frightening situation.

"We should tell them we're students," I told Laura. "We're studying at UCLA film school and Mitch is our professor." She nodded in agreement.

"Where is her coat?" the officer asked the soldier guarding us, gesturing toward me.

"She doesn't have one," the soldier answered. I hoped this meant that he didn't realize I'd left it at the river—otherwise, they might go back to retrieve it. Within a few minutes, someone brought me an army overcoat to wear, and the soldier guarding us gave me a rag to wipe the blood from Laura's face. In their own way, they seemed to be trying to look after us, and I took some comfort from that. I had genuinely feared they might kill us, but they were treating us with some kindness, which surprised and confused me.

After a few more minutes, the officer finally led us into the gray building. He walked us into a small room, about ten feet by ten feet, that was apparently his office. It was very spare, with only an old wooden desk and chair, and two chairs set up for Laura and me.

As I sat in one of the chairs, I was overcome with the strange feeling that I'd been here before. Even looking at the handwritten name tag on the officer's desk, I felt like I recognized his name from somewhere. I'd never experienced déjà vu before, but Michael had told me about it, and I realized this must be what it felt like. I couldn't possibly have ever been in this office or seen this man before, yet everything was eerily familiar.

I turned to Laura and said, "I'm sorry, but it feels like we're supposed to be here. I've seen this before." Laura didn't respond, but I'm sure my comment confused her. I knew it didn't make any sense, but the feeling was so strong, it felt almost like I was in a movie. If things had seemed surreal before, they felt even more so now.

As we sat watching nervously, the officer began looking through my backpack. I tried to remember everything that was in it: my passport, wallet with ID and credit cards, American dollars and Chinese yuan, two Ziploc bags of baby wipes, a pair of pajama pants, bread, chocolate. I also had my U.S. cell phone, which I wasn't using in Asia but had brought along so I'd have photos of Hana and Michael with me. And there were a few more videotapes—footage we'd shot while in China.

The officer, a tall man with kind eyes, held up my passport and said, "So. You're Americans?"

"Yes," I said. "We're students."

"Why were you out on the river?" he asked.

"We were just following our professor," I said, knowing that the soldiers had seen Mitch with us there. Because the officer's demeanor was gentle, I hoped he would have mercy on us and let us go. Or maybe he was even one of the border guards our guide knew? I had to believe that the officer would understand the situation and let us return. Surely that would be best for everyone—wouldn't it?

The tall officer said nothing for a few minutes and sat at his desk writing. He was very calm, and though he didn't seem angry with us, he had a worried look on his face. Eventually, the tall officer gave an order to a second officer, who escorted us out of the building. Incredibly, some part of my brain at this point was still in editor mode. "Remember everything you're seeing!" I said to Laura, thinking we could include a firsthand view of what North Korea was like in our documentary. And Laura must have been thinking the same thing, because she answered, "Remember the slogans on the buildings," since she herself couldn't read them.

As we stood outside, the tall officer showed us a list he'd made of our possessions and the amount of money we were carrying, and read the list aloud for me to confirm the items. Then the second officer, along with the two soldiers who'd captured us, began walking us to another location. I didn't like the idea of going anywhere else, figuring that as long as we were near the border we had a better chance of being released quickly. But the order had been given, so Laura and I traipsed along with the soldiers and officer, walking deeper into the countryside. The officer had taken back the army coat, and because it was still early in the morning—perhaps about 7:30 A.M.—I was exposed to the cold again, in my wet pants and sweater. Disoriented from trying to take everything in, I hardly noticed.

So many thoughts, some of them crazy, were racing through my mind. As the soldiers marched us up and down the hillsides, I saw a man tending a small herd of goats. A strange idea flashed into my mind: Maybe he was a spy for the Chinese, here to keep tabs on what was happening to us? Was he some kind of agent, sent to help us get back safely? I searched for any sliver of hope that our ordeal would be over soon, as I simply couldn't grasp the alternative.

We walked and walked, and around every bend the officer kept saying, "We're almost there!" After about twenty minutes, we finally arrived at our destination—another military installation. Like the first base, this one was little more than a collection of small, gray, utilitarian buildings. But we also saw something that seemed straight out of the 1940s: a motorcycle with a sidecar, like the kind you see in World War II movies.

To our surprise, the officer instructed Laura and me to climb into the two-seat sidecar. I got in the front and Laura was behind me. As we settled in, he asked, "Where do you want to go? To the border?" Was he kidding?

"Please, please take us to the border!" I said, and part of me believed he really would do it. I translated the exchange for Laura, and both of us were on the edge of our seats as the officer hopped on the motorcycle.

"Don't worry," he said. "It'll be okay." He started up the motorcycle and began to pull out, with a hearty "Let's go!"

If I hadn't felt the cold before, I really felt it now, with the wind whipping in my face and the damp in my clothes turning to ice. Within minutes of leaving the base, I couldn't feel my ears.

After a short time on the road, we passed a sign written in Chinese and I realized it must be the name of a village near the border with China. We were so close—if the driver just made a right turn into that village, we could cross back over into China and this nightmare would be over! I said a silent prayer, desperate for the driver to turn toward the village—and just then an army jeep pulled up, stopping the motorcycle.

The jeep's driver talked for a few minutes with our officer, but I couldn't hear what they were saying. Then the officer climbed back on and started the motorcycle again, and again my spirits soared—were they going to set us free? But instead of turning right to go to the village, the motorcycle turned left, heading directly away from China and deeper into North

Korea. I felt crushed, more scared than ever, and guilty for having gotten Laura's hopes up. I really had thought we'd be okay, but now I had no idea what fate awaited us.

❀

After twenty or thirty minutes on the road, we arrived at a third military installation. My face and ears were numb from the cold, and I was shivering so hard it was difficult to climb out of the sidecar. By now, Laura and I had been in North Korean custody for several hours, and we were tired and scared.

The officer escorted us into a building, then asked us to take off our shoes before showing us into a small room with a yellow vinyl floor. The walls were covered in cheap-looking, flowery wallpaper that looked like Korean country decor from the 1980s—like the wallpaper in my grandmother's house.

As foreign and frightening as this day had been so far, it was strange to now be put in a room that so reminded me of my childhood. In the 1980s, while I was in elementary school, my grandma still lived in the traditional-style Korean wood house where my dad had grown up. We always visited her during summer breaks from school, and I remember vividly her faded wallpaper, antique furniture, and wall clocks. Seeing the wallpaper and vinyl flooring in this room perfectly summed up the oddness of being held captive in North Korea—things seemed familiar and unfamiliar at the same time.

Laura and I sat on the floor, where a comforter and blan-ket had been placed, and officers began coming in and out of the room, asking questions. They asked who we were and what we were doing at the river, and we told them all the same thing: that we were students taking film classes at UCLA and we had been at the river with our professor. One asked if we'd had any breakfast, and when I said no, he remarked, "Well, it's almost the lunch hour anyway." After a while, they brought us some soup and a sticky rice dish, but neither Laura nor I ate much. We were too freaked out to have any appetite.

While we were in the room, an officer brought us my backpack and Laura's tote bag. Another walked in with Lau-ra's camera and asked us to show him how it worked. She took it and began showing him, surreptitiously managing to delete some photos while she did it. Laura had taken still pho-tos and video with the camera over the last ten days, and she knew there were images of the defectors we had interviewed. So she worked fast, deleting photos in front of the oblivious officer as he tried to understand how the camera worked.

Another officer had been looking through Laura's iPod—they all seemed fascinated by our machines—but somehow it had gotten locked. He asked for the password, and I trans-lated the request for her. But Laura said she had never locked it, so she wasn't sure what the password was. We tried several combinations of letters and digits, but no one could figure out how to unlock it. "There's nothing to hide in there, just family pictures and music," Laura said. "You can break it if you think that'll unlock it." The officer left the room, taking the iPod with him.

At some point the other officers left us alone in the room, and although they were holding on to our cameras and the iPod, we still had our bags. "My notebook is in here," Laura told me, "and it's got the questions I wrote down when I interviewed Pastor Chun. Should I get rid of them?"

"Yes," I said. "Let's do it, fast."

She tore a page and a half out of the notebook—not only the interview questions for Pastor Chun, but a half-page with the phone number of one of our contacts, too. "What should we do with them?" she asked. We considered hiding them under the vinyl floor covering, but they would almost certainly be found there. So I crumpled up the page with the phone number and swallowed it, and Laura crumpled the page of interview notes, stuffed it into an empty gum packet, and put it in the bottom of her bag.

The officers still hadn't returned, so I decided to do something about the tapes, too. Some were blank, but the ones that had footage had labels on them. I said to Laura, "You can tell which ones are used because of the labels. Should I take them off?"

"Yes," she said. "But be careful." She was worried we'd be caught doing it, so she acted as a lookout, keeping her eye on the door while I worked as quickly as I could.

I peeled the labels off the two used tapes, tore them into

tiny pieces, and stuffed them into the bottom of my backpack. We were still alone in the room, so I decided to sabotage the tapes themselves, too. I pulled up the protective covers and ripped each tape in half so the camera couldn't read them. I did this for both tapes that had footage on them, hoping that the North Koreans wouldn't figure out that they could repair and view them.

We finished sabotaging the tapes, and as we sat in the room waiting for someone to come, the tension became almost unbearable. Laura was really worried that something terrible might happen to us—that we might never make it back home. I felt surprisingly calm at that moment, so I wanted to comfort her but didn't know how. Then I remembered Michael's dream.

"Laura," I said, "I don't know if this will make you feel better, but I want to tell you about a dream Michael had." It had happened before Hana was born: Michael dreamed he was visiting me in the hospital, where I had just given birth to our second child. He walked in holding hands with a little girl—a girl he would later realize was Hana. He described how happy he felt in the dream, seeing me with our new baby and holding hands with our daughter. Michael believed his dream would come true, and I did, too. This belief was so strong, it would end up sustaining me through even my darkest hours in North Korea.

"When Hana had to have surgery," I told Laura, "we didn't know if she would be okay. But I remembered that dream, and it gave me peace. We'll get back home, Laura. We have to, because I haven't had that second baby yet!"

I had hoped to reassure her, even as I was reassuring myself, but instead she sat in silence. After a few minutes, she turned to me with a concerned look on her face. "Euna," she said, "*I'm* not in Michael's dream."

I felt terrible. I had meant to comfort Laura, but instead I'd only made her more nervous. I wanted to put her mind at ease, but clearly I didn't know how. We sat in silence until eventually a female soldier came in.

"What's going to happen to us?" I asked the soldier. "Are we going home?"

"Don't worry," she said. "Everything will be okay." At this point, we weren't sure whether anyone even knew we were missing. Had Mitch made it back to safety? Had he told the U.S. authorities that we had been captured? What would happen once the U.S. government learned we were in North Korean custody—would they be able to get us released?

The uncertainty of our situation was nerve-racking, but at each new location we were at least able to find some small comfort in getting accustomed to our surroundings. So far, most of the officers had been relatively kind, though a few snapped and glared at us. The worst moments came when things suddenly changed, as it felt like whatever came next would probably be worse than what we had experienced so far. Each time the North Koreans moved us, it seemed we were getting farther away from the possibility of a quick release.

To my dismay, about an hour after we had settled into this wallpapered room, an officer told us we were moving again. This made me nervous, but what happened next made it worse: A soldier took two handkerchiefs out of Laura's bag and used them to blindfold us.

A female soldier said, "Hold my hand." I took her hand and Laura took mine, and the soldier led us out of the building. "If there's any steps up or down, I'll warn you," she said. I translated her words for Laura, and we shuffled along behind the soldier, scared out of our wits. Why were they blindfolding us? Were they going to shoot us? Were they taking us somewhere we'd never be found?

She walked us out of the building and through an exercise yard, and I could hear soldiers shouting. We were led into another building, and someone removed our blindfolds. A male soldier was in the room, and he asked, "Did you understand what the men in the yard were saying?"

"No," I answered. "Did you want me to?"

"No," he replied. "You're going to be taken to another location," he went on, "so you may want to use the bathroom." I was grateful for the chance to go, but because the bathroom was outside the building, the female soldier blindfolded us again for the walk. Back in the room, I decided to change out of the pants I had on. They were still damp and dirty from being dragged on the ice, so I put on the pair of pajama pants I had in my backpack—sky-blue fleece pants with polka dots. It felt strange to be wearing pajamas, but then again, the whole situation was so strange that nothing could possibly feel normal.

The soldier blindfolded us yet again and led us outside the building to a waiting car. She put us in the back seat, and I could feel to my horror that someone was handcuffing my wrist to Laura's. Laura and I sat there shaking, holding hands tightly, as two men piled into the back seat, one on either side of us. By now I was terrified, and I began crying for the first time in this whole ordeal. I just couldn't believe that any of this was really happening.

We were in the car for about one hour, jostling along a pot-holed road and feeling every bump. Neither Laura nor I spoke, and I couldn't see anything at all through the blindfold—it was a strange sensation to be so cut off from the world. We gripped each other's hands the whole time and I tried not to give in to the panic that was rising in my chest. Finally, the car shuddered to a stop and someone took the handcuffs off our wrists. We were pulled from the car, still blindfolded and with no idea where we were.

Right away, I could feel that this place was different from the others. Someone pushed me roughly from behind and barked, "Go in there!" From that moment, I had no idea what happened to Laura; I was now alone with my captors. On every side, people were shouting orders, and I tried to follow them. I stumbled into some kind of building. After walking a short distance, I heard a voice say, "Stop!" At the same time, someone reached up and yanked off my blindfold.

It took a moment for my eyes to adjust in the half-light, and when they did, I felt a stab of fear. I was looking at a prison cell.

❖

The cell was tiny—about five feet by seven feet, just about big enough for two people to lie down side by side. I could see a small bed made of wooden slats, with blankets, and a bare lightbulb hanging from the ceiling. There was a tiny window with bars on it, but it was too high up to see through. And the heavy, gray steel door had just two small, rectangular openings with sliding doors—one for the guards to look in and one for meal trays to slide through.

A soldier led me in, then turned and left, locking the heavy door behind him. I felt as though I couldn't breathe—there was no source of air. All I could think was, *I'm in a cell. I'm a prisoner.* And as far as I could tell, no one but a handful of North Koreans knew we were even here.

Outside my cell, two soldiers—one short, one tall—stood guard. Directly behind the desk where they sat was a second metal-bar gate, which could only be opened with a key. There was clearly no way to escape this prison.

One of the guards pushed a stainless-steel bowl of food through the small opening in my door. It was some kind of grain—barley, or maybe oatmeal—with little bits of something yellow and pieces of kimchi mixed in. I managed to take a couple of bites but couldn't swallow any more. It wasn't that the dish tasted bad—I just was too upset and scared to eat. After a while, a guard peered into the cell. "Why didn't you finish?" he asked. "Was it bad?"

"No," I said, hoping he wouldn't be offended, as if I were a dinner guest rather than a prisoner. "I just don't have an appetite." But no sooner had he taken the bowl away than I thought, *What if they don't bring me any more food? I should have eaten it!*

Alone in my cell, with nothing but four blank walls to look at and not enough room to walk around, I couldn't stop my mind from racing. I'm the kind of person who prefers to just keep moving, rather than sitting and contemplating things. Thinking too much always makes me nervous, and the more I sat there thinking, the more scared I got. I started crying, desperate to get out but knowing I couldn't—and so frightened it didn't even occur to me to pray and ask for God's help.

Sometime that afternoon, the guard unlocked my cell door and swung it open. A short, chubby officer, maybe about fifty years old, was standing there. "Come with me," he said, and I gratefully stepped out of the cell. They had taken my shoes, and I was wearing only socks. The guard gestured at the black slippers—footwear for prisoners—outside my cell. I put them on and followed him down the hallway, staring at my feet.

He showed me into a room with a big desk and told me to sit in the chair facing it. I did, and he walked around and took a seat behind it. On top of the desk were my camera and tapes.

"What were you doing at the river?" the officer asked.

"I'm a student," I said. "I followed my professor there." I told him the same story we had told the other officers: that Laura and I were studying film at UCLA and that we were working on a class project.

The officer just glared at me. "You're not a student," he said. "You're a spy. Does your 'professor' work with the CIA? The FBI? Why were you at that part of the river? Were you shooting that footage for the government?"

"No, no!" I told him. "We just wanted to look. We did a similar project about the U.S. and Mexico, examining how business is conducted across the border." Because we'd been captured at the border between North Korea and China, I knew I had to make up a believable story explaining why we were in that particular place. I kept talking, going on about how China's economy was changing and how we wanted to explore the ways people did business across international lines. But the officer seemed to know I was lying. He stared at me through his thick glasses and continued to pepper me with questions.

The interrogation went on for hours, into the evening and then night. He kept asking questions, and I wouldn't budge from my story. Laura and I were students, Mitch was our professor, and we didn't mean to break any rules or laws. Back and forth and back and forth we went, and my interrogator was growing frustrated. Another officer came in and said, "Laura is telling us everything! You are telling us nothing! If you don't tell us the truth, you're going to a worse place than that cell!" It was the first time, but not the last, that the North Koreans would try to use Laura and me against each other to get more information.

"I am telling the truth," I said. "There's nothing else to tell." I didn't believe that Laura was revealing anything more than what we had discussed, no matter what the officers said. And I was determined not to give up on the story we'd agreed on.

At one point, the interrogator held up the tapes he'd found in my backpack. "We know what you did," he said. "Everything was recorded on your camera. You want to see?" He pushed the camera across the desk to me. I shuddered and shook my head. I knew the camera had been running when we were captured, and I didn't want to relive that moment.

"Play the tape," the interrogator said. Shaking, I pushed the play button, and as we watched on the viewfinder, we saw Laura doing her standup on the river that morning, saying our guide had just crossed the border. There was also a brief clip of the guide, filmed from the back.

"Who is he?" the interrogator demanded.

"Our driver," I said.

The interrogator looked doubtful, but he had no way to disprove me, so he said nothing. As I pushed a few other buttons on the camera, he barked, "Are you getting rid of the evidence?"

"No," I said, "I'm not." And I wasn't—but as it turned out, the interrogator himself had erased part of the tape, accidentally filming me sitting across the desk from him. And incredibly enough, he happened to erase the few seconds where I had inadvertently filmed the guide's face when he suddenly turned toward me at the river. I was never so relieved to see video footage of myself.

The interrogator instructed me to find more footage on the other tapes, since he didn't know how to use the camera. There were six tapes altogether—four blank ones and the two that I had damaged at the military base. I inserted the blank ones and showed the interrogator that there was nothing on them. And when I inserted the tapes I had damaged, I hit the fast-forward button to pull them deeper into the cassette casing. The camera showed an error message, and I said, "There's nothing here." To my relief, he seemed to believe me.

He put the tapes aside and resumed questioning me. For several more hours, he tried to get me to change my story, and although he never threatened me physically, his demeanor became more menacing as the time ticked by. He accused me of being a spy, or at least working for a spy, and I insisted that I wasn't. I stuck to my story, and gradually he began to realize he wasn't going to get anywhere. So he tried a different tack.

"Write down everything you've been telling me," he said, pushing a pen and some paper across the table.

I started to write, and the next time I looked up, I saw to my surprise that my interrogator had fallen asleep at his desk. I glanced at a clock on the wall—it was after 3:30 A.M.! I had been in this interrogation room for about eight hours, and awake for almost twenty-four hours, ever since getting up the previous morning to go to the Tumen River.

As the clock hands swept toward 4 A.M., I was finally led back to my cell. Hearing the big metal door clank shut behind me, I wondered what could possibly happen next. I hoped Mitch had made it to safety and reported our situation, but beyond that there wasn't much to be optimistic about. Would the North Koreans just keep us in this prison until we gave in and claimed to be spies? And would it be better for us, or worse, to do what they asked? I was paralyzed with uncertainty, fearing that if I made the wrong decision now about whether to tell the truth, I might regret it forever.

I was scared and exhausted and had never felt so alone. But as I lay down in the bed and inhaled the smell of the wood the guards burned to keep the dank cells warm, I was reminded once again of my grandmother's house in South Korea. She often burned wood for cooking and heating, and I remembered sitting next to her in the kitchen while she fanned the flames. Despite my fear, I found the smell comforting, and eventually I fell asleep.

❖

Just a few hours later, the guard shouted into my cell. "Wake up," he said. "Sit tight." I didn't know what was coming— more interrogation? Would I see Laura? I hadn't seen her since we arrived at this place, and I had no idea where she was.

After an hour or so, the guard opened my door and said, "Come with me." I followed him to a small room just off the guards' area, and when I walked in I saw a frightening scene. Laura was there, screaming my name while a man next to her held a pair of forceps over an open flame. For a brief moment I thought she was somehow being tortured, but then I quickly realized they were sterilizing the forceps to help clean the wound on her forehead. Here was another sight out of the past, like the motorcycle sidecars and 1980s wallpaper, that confirmed my impression of North Korea as a place suspended in time.

The men in the room were apparently medical professionals, but none of them spoke English. Unsure of what was happening, Laura had called my name over and over until they brought me into the room.

"Tell her we're cleaning her wound so it doesn't get infected," one of the men said. I translated his words for Laura, and she seemed relieved.

"I thought as much," she said, "but I wasn't sure."

"Are you doing okay?" I asked, relieved to be seeing her again. "How are you feeling?"

She said, "I'm okay," then asked me how her head looked. The truth was, it looked horrible—the wound was jagged and looked like it hadn't closed properly. But I didn't want her to worry, so I said, "It looks clean. It will be fine." The guards discouraged us from talking more, so I just translated whatever the medical people needed to tell Laura. After they finished dressing her wound, the guards took us back to our cells, and I realized for the first time that Laura was being kept in the cell right next to mine.

I was glad to have Laura so close by, and also happy to discover that the guards' demeanor was different this morning. When they brought breakfast, instead of sliding it through the small opening, they just opened our cell doors. And the food was better than that the day before—not only rice, but side dishes of tofu, kimchi, and boiled egg, too.

With our cell doors open, Laura and I were able to talk to each other, though the guards discouraged it. And we found other ways to communicate, too. Though one of the guards spoke a little English, he couldn't understand Laura's questions, so he'd ask for my help translating them. I'd translate what he asked, then slip in other comments to Laura whenever I could. And although the guards wouldn't allow Laura and me to go to the bathroom at the same time, whenever I went down the hall to the bathroom I walked right by Laura's cell door, so we could quickly exchange a few words then.

In this way, Laura and I were able to communicate at least a little bit. I was so worried about her—worried about her head wound, the painful stomach ulcer I knew she had, and the fear she must be feeling in a place where she couldn't even understand the language. As difficult as all this was for me, at least I spoke Korean. I wanted to offer Laura what little comfort I could, especially when I heard her crying in her cell.

Fear of something you know can be scary, but the fear of the unknown is terrifying.

At lunchtime the same day, a short, stout man who had apparently been in the room during Laura's interrogation came to my cell to ask me some questions.

"You say you and Laura are graduate students," he said. "How many people are in your class?"

If I answered something completely different from Laura, they would know for sure we were lying. But how could I possibly know what she had said? "Laura and I are at a different level," I responded. "I started two years after she did." But the man wasn't taking that for an answer.

"So how many students are in your class?" he pressed, baring his gold-capped teeth in a sarcastic smile. "And how many Asians?"

I was afraid to answer—afraid that whatever I said in this moment might seal our fate for the worse. But I had no choice. I had to say something, so I thought for a moment and randomly picked a number. "About eighteen to twenty-five students," I said, "and two Asians." I hoped that by some miracle Laura had said the same thing. The man studied me for a moment, his face like stone. Then he turned and left.

Because it was lunchtime, our cell doors were open. Speaking quickly, I said, "Laura! Did he ask you how many people are in our class?" The guards could hear us, but even the one who spoke some English couldn't understand what we were saying if we spoke fast.

She answered immediately. "I told them sixteen," she said, and for a moment my heart soared. "And five Asians." Just like that, my hopes sank. Our answers didn't match, which meant they would know we were lying. We were trapped. What could we do now?

The next time I went down the hallway to the bathroom, Laura asked, "Euna, should we tell them we work for Current? They think we are spies." I didn't answer her right away, but kept going down the hall. I was so torn, wondering whether we'd make things worse by revealing who we were. But increasingly, it seemed we didn't have a choice. They were going to find out one way or another.

On the way back from the bathroom, I passed Laura's cell again. And again I heard her voice: "Euna, do you think we should tell them?" This time, I answered. "Okay," I said. "Let's tell them we work for Current. But not about the specific story we were working on."

When an officer came to take me back to the interrogation room, I said, "Okay, we're ready to tell you everything. But we want to do it together."

"We can't do that," he said. "You must be in separate rooms."

"Laura said her interpreter isn't good," I countered. "We will only do it if we can be together. I will translate for her." We didn't really have any leverage to make demands, but this military installation obviously had limited resources, and I was the best available translator. To my relief, the officer relented, saying that I could translate for Laura but I had to make my statement first—alone. The guards opened our cell doors, and the officer walked me down to the same room where I had been interrogated the day before.

I took a deep breath and began. "We work for a network called Current TV," I told them. "We were doing a story about the China–North Korea border, comparing it to the one between Mexico and the United States." I said that we had come to the river to shoot footage for our network, and that we were covering how the Chinese economy was affecting the border—but I said nothing about North Korean defectors, knowing it would anger them to find out what the documentary was really about.

When I had finished, the guard walked me down the hallway to another room, this one with a sofa, table, and TV. It looked like a lounge for the officers, but this was the room where Laura would make her statement.

One of the officers said to me, "You have to be honest in your translation. Don't change anything." He then turned to Laura. "Why were you at the river?"

Laura said something similar to what I'd said, and I translated it to be almost exactly the same. The officers told us to write down our statements, and we did—mine in Korean, Laura's in English. Much of what I wrote was true—my name, age, title at Current TV, the fact that Mitch was my producer. But I also wrote that we were working on a border story and that a taxi driver had brought us to the river, neither of which was true. I also asked forgiveness for having crossed the border, which I hoped would gain us some lenience.

As I wrote, I glanced at the officers' faces, and it was obvious they were happy we had finally come clean. Maybe this was all they needed? A simple acknowledgment that we were journalists? I dared to hope that this was the key—that maybe the North Koreans would let us go now.

After we'd finished our statements, Laura asked if she and I could stay in the same cell that night. I doubted they would allow it, but I translated her request to the short, chubby officer—and to my surprise, he said yes. Surely this was a good sign—why would they grant us a request if they didn't feel favorably about us? This would be our second night in North Korea, and with any luck maybe it would be our last.

❧

Back in my cell, Laura and I talked about everything that had happened and what might happen next. We still didn't know whether revealing we were journalists had been the right move, but so far it didn't seem to have hurt us. Laura was now more worried than ever about the crumpled-up page of interview notes at the bottom of her bag. She wanted to destroy it completely so the North Koreans wouldn't find out we had interviewed Pastor Chun.

I asked the guards if she could have her bag, telling them she needed some "female products" that were in it. They asked us to step out of the cell and handed her the bag, keeping an eye on her as she rummaged through it. Despite their surveillance, she managed to grab the wad of paper along with a compact and lotion.

When we got back to our cell, she seemed unsure of how to get rid of it. I took the paper from her hand and tore it in half, putting one half in my mouth and handing the other to her. She stuck the paper in her mouth, too, but while I chewed and swallowed mine, she suddenly got a funny look on her face and took hers out. She had remembered her ulcer and was afraid that eating paper might inflame it. So instead she put the chewed-up wad of paper in her pocket. I don't know what she did with it after that, but to my knowledge the guards never saw it.

I felt relieved to be together with Laura rather than alone in my silent cell. We weren't particularly close before the trip—I liked her as a colleague but didn't really know her personally. We had met in 2005 when I started at Current, but we rarely worked together until I joined the Vanguard division. That night, we talked about our families and our lives back home. She told me about how she and her husband Iain had met, and I told her about Michael, and about Hana's heart surgeries. We spent long stretches in silence, too, lost in our own thoughts.

When we talked about our families, we talked freely. But when we talked about anything we didn't want the North Koreans to know, we used our fingers to trace letters on the cell floor. We both knew that if we mentioned Pastor Chun it would endanger not only us but also North Korean defectors. I wrote "Pastor Chun" on the floor with my finger and said "no." She nodded. Then I wrote "Driver?"—meaning our guide. She shook her head—"no." We also agreed that if the interrogations continued we still wouldn't reveal anything about the true nature of our documentary. So far the North Koreans didn't have evidence to prove what we were doing, and we wanted to keep it that way.

We also talked about what the chances were that we might be released sooner rather than later. I told Laura I hoped that the media back home wouldn't find out we had been captured, as it seemed better for us if negotiations could go on in secret. Once the story broke, it might become a bigger issue between the two countries, especially since we worked for Al Gore's TV station.

At one point, Laura noticed some Korean writing scratched into the cell wall. "What does it say?" she asked. I leaned close. "I miss my mom," I read aloud. And there was another: "Keep the spirit up. If you lose spirit, you'll lose everything." I wondered who had been kept in this cell before us, and why. And, of course, I couldn't help but wonder—for how long?

That night, Laura gave me a massage to help me relax. She also showed me some yoga techniques, saying, "We should keep moving. It's better for us." I taught her some Korean that would be useful for her in case we were separated again, including phrases such as "Water, please," "I need to use the bathroom," "I am sick," and "Please get Euna for me." When we finally slept, I slept well—Laura even teased me the next morning that I snored all night.

When breakfast came the next day, Laura said, "Let's eat slowly," since the guards would leave our cell door open until they retrieved our trays. As with the night before, she and I didn't talk much, because we were lost in our own thoughts. I tried not to think about what the day would bring, but just pushed all the questions out of my head as best I could. We'd find out soon enough what would happen to us, and anyway, there was nothing we could do to change it.

After breakfast, an officer came to take Laura and me back into the interrogation room. He handed us each a set of stapled papers, consisting of our handwritten statements and officially typed copies. "These are your confessions," he said. Then he pushed an ink pad toward us. "You will put your fingerprints on them."

Laura and I both burst into tears. Confessions? Would they use these to keep us in prison forever? Or even execute us? I knew from my research that the North Korean government showed no mercy to criminals—and if we put our finger-prints to these documents, it meant we were admitting that's what we were. But what choice did we have? Our captors had the tape in my camera, which showed we had walked onto North Korean soil. If we refused to sign a confession, our pun-ishment might be even worse.

Before, I had let myself hope that we might be released

quickly. But now I feared that the worst was really in front of us. We were about to become confessed criminals—and once they had our confessions, there was nothing we could do to take them back.

"Euna," Laura suddenly said, "I'm only going to say this once. You have a daughter. Tell them to let you go, and I will stay here for you." I turned to her in surprise. It was a very generous suggestion, but there was no way I could let her take my place. Already, in just two days, we had been through so much together—I couldn't leave her by herself here. "No, Laura," I told her. "We will go home together."

One by one, we pressed our ink-stained fingers to the documents, tears streaming down our faces. I shuddered, deeply shaken by a feeling that they might actually kill us after we confessed. There was something very dark about this place, and I was gripped by a terrible sense of foreboding. But it was too late to do anything now—we had confessed to a crime.

The guards started to take us back to the cell, but suddenly the chubby officer said, "Why don't you clean yourselves?" We hadn't bathed since before we'd been captured, so despite feeling completely miserable about our situation, I welcomed the chance to clean up. The guards took us to the lounge where Laura had given her statement, and showed us to the attached bathroom.

But this was no relaxing bath—far from it. The water was freezing, so Laura and I cleaned up as quickly as we could. I washed her hair, trying to keep water from getting into the wound on her forehead. We hurried to get ourselves washed up before our hands went numb, but despite the cold, it felt like a wonderful luxury to be able to clean ourselves.

The guards told us we would be moving to yet another location, and at lunch I asked the tall officer whether we would be sent home. "It will take about two weeks," he said, "and then you will be home." I didn't believe him, though, especially after he indicated that our next destination was Pyongyang. As long as we were near the border, it might be possible to release us without any kind of incident. But if we were sent to Pyongyang, that meant higher levels of the North Korean government were involved, and the stakes became that much higher. I was upset about the relocation and upset that the officer was apparently lying to me, despite how much I wanted to believe him. However bad this all had been, it now seemed possible that worse was yet to come.

Now that it was clear we weren't going home, Laura and I took a step that seemed drastic but necessary: We shared messages for each other's family, in case something happened to one of us.

I won't reveal what Laura said, as it's hers to share, not mine. But the message I gave to her was the first thing that popped into my head. "Tell Michael it's okay if he remarries," I said. "He should do what's right for Hana." Laura and I held hands tightly and cried, and I wondered what could possibly happen next.

Five

GETTING TO PYONGYANG

B<small>Y NOW</small>, Laura and I had been in North Korean custody for more than forty-eight hours. I'd hardly eaten anything, as my stomach was tied in a big, nervous knot. So when I put back on my brown corduroy pants after the guards had dried them, I realized with shock that I had already lost weight.

At around 4 in the afternoon, the guards showed Laura and me to a waiting car that would take us to yet another location—our fifth so far. One officer climbed into the back seat with us while two others sat in front, and I was relieved they had decided not to handcuff or blindfold us, though one of the officers did ask us to close our eyes. I did as I was told, but opened my eyes again as soon as I could. I was afraid of not knowing where we were, and I tried to remember the route back to the border even though my sense of direction is terrible.

After about a three-hour drive, we arrived at a building that looked like a motel. It wasn't like a normal motel, though—there were no guests that I could see, only the people who worked there. The officers showed Laura and me to our rooms, which were clean and comfortable despite their old-style furnishings, including a black-and-white TV with an antenna. Then they gave us a menu and invited us to choose what we wanted for dinner.

The atmosphere at this motel was much more relaxed than that at the military bases. As we ate, the officers talked with us, even making jokes about the situation we were in. "You didn't check your fortune for this year, did you?" one asked with a smile. "No, I didn't," I answered, even smiling a little myself. Although I was scared about where we were heading and what awaited us there, it was a relief to have a human connection with these officers rather than the harshness of interrogation.

"You thought we were all red-faced monsters, huh?" another officer asked, referring to South Koreans' impressions of North Koreans.

"No," I said, "I think you guys are really nice." To my surprise, despite our situation, I really did feel that way about most of the North Koreans we had met so far.

I thought back on what I'd learned about North Koreans as a child in Seoul. The Cold War was in full force then, and the South Korean government routinely bombarded its citizens with anti–North Korea propaganda. I remembered in particular a cartoon I had watched in which a boy's father is kidnapped by North Koreans. The boy heroically tries to defeat North Korean spies to get his father back, and then-leader Kim Il-sung is depicted as a fat, squealing pig in a red cloak.

I realized I had bought into the stereotypes of North Koreans wholeheartedly, never really thinking about the fact that they were people like me—fellow Koreans who just happened to live under a different political system. Because of our situation and the strange stuck-in-time quality of North Korea, they still seemed very foreign to me, but they weren't really as different as I always had thought.

The officers tried to make sure we were taken care of, sending a doctor in after dinner to check on Laura's head wound. I told the doctor that Laura and I had been suffering from diarrhea ever since our lunch of cold noodles at the last military base, and after asking a few questions, he gave us a powder wrapped in paper.

"Take this," he said. "It will help."

I wasn't very happy about taking medicine from a doctor I didn't know, but I swallowed the powder anyway. When it hit my stomach, I felt like a fire had been lit inside me. It was frightening for a few moments, but eventually the feeling wore off. And to my surprise, the powder seemed to work— my digestive system got back on track that night.

It was a relief to be in a comfortable room rather than a

cold jail cell, but even so, as I tried to fall asleep, my mind felt numb. The farther we were taken from the border, the more helpless I felt about my situation. It was impossible to know what would come next, so I decided just to face it whenever it came. I closed my eyes and my mind shut down. I slept.

❈

The next morning, our fourth day in captivity, I asked the officer who was guarding me if I could look out the window of my room. We had arrived late at night when it was pitch black outside, but I was curious to see where we were in the daylight. He said I could look, and I slowly pulled back the curtain.

The scene outside was beautiful. There were train tracks running through the freshly fallen snow, and just beyond the tracks was a small village, a collection of old-style mud-brick houses with shingled roofs and smoke curling lazily out of chimneys. Villagers walked along through the snow, some of them pushing bikes, just living their everyday lives. It was like a movie set—a perfectly constructed picture of tranquillity. Nothing had felt normal since Laura and I were captured, but here, for the first time, it was possible to imagine that North Korea was like anyplace else.

Then I saw a little boy, about three years old, bundled up in his winter coat and hat. He walked out of a house with an adult, maybe a parent, but as I watched, he walked by himself to the corner of the house and stood there, waiting. Looking at him, I felt a pang deep in my stomach—he looked so small and alone standing there waiting. He reminded me so much of Hana, who was waiting for me at home.

I had tried not to think about Hana since we had been captured, as every time I did I couldn't stop my tears from flowing. I missed her, but even more than that, I felt terrible for having put myself in the situation I was in. What kind of mother puts herself in danger like I had? What was I doing? I thought about how shocked Michael would be when he found out what had happened, and how his distress would affect Hana. Every time I thought about the promise I had made Hana to come home, I felt suffocated with guilt. There was still a chance I could make it home by the date I had promised, but now that Laura and I were apparently being taken to Pyongyang, the possibility seemed more and more remote.

Late that afternoon, we got back into the car and set out again. We rode for a couple of hours, as the terrain grew hillier and then mountainous. The roads weren't very good, and the farther we went the fewer signs of life we saw. Finally, just as we appeared to be in the middle of nowhere, the driver pulled the car over and the man in the back seat with us said, "Why don't you get out?"

We were on the side of a mountain, with a steep cliff drop-off to one side. Laura got out and said, "It feels so good to get some fresh air!" The driver had popped the hood and was looking at the engine, and I got out of the car too, relieved to stretch my legs.

It was absolutely quiet, and no one else was around. All of a sudden, I thought, *They've brought us here to kill us! They're going to throw us over the cliff's edge, where no one will ever find us!* Why else would they have stopped in this place? Why else would they have invited us to get out of the car specifically here?

Shaking with fear, I got right back into the car. Laura, who was still standing outside, said, "Euna, what are you doing? Don't you want some fresh air?"

"I don't feel like being outside," I told her, my heart racing. I didn't explain why, as I didn't want to frighten her, but I did urge her to get back in the car. My feeling was, the car was the only safe place to be, because they couldn't do anything to me as long as I was in it. I didn't know if I was being paranoid or not, but the fear was real.

I nervously watched Laura from the back seat, and it was a big relief when she got back in. "I think I've watched too many movies," I said as she got in beside me.

The driver and the officers got back in and we continued on. We stopped briefly for dinner around 8 P.M.—the main officer apologized that we were eating so late—then got right back on the road. I fell asleep during the drive, and after a few hours we stopped at a building by the side of the road. The officers said we could use the bathroom here, but when we got out of the car we saw two sedans waiting. "Oh no," Laura said. "They're separating us."

As much as I had feared being separated from Laura, I felt surprisingly calm. I told myself that this might even be good for her. Had the North Koreans decided they didn't need to keep us both? Were they sending Laura home and keeping me because I could speak Korean? I hoped they would send at least one of us home—but as with everything else, it was impossible to know what the North Koreans had in mind for us.

The officers put me into one of the sedans first, with two of them in the front seat and two more in the back, one on either side of me, and we left. I had no idea when I would see Laura again. I hoped it would be at home. As it turned out, we were reunited two and a half months later—in a Pyongyang courtroom at our trial in June.

I tried to stay awake as we rode through North Korea's mountainous northern region, but as the clock ticked deep into the night, I grew more and more tired. The officers had told me to close my eyes during the trip, but occasionally I would sneak a glimpse out the window. I had thought the entire ride would take about six or seven hours, because that's about how long it takes to drive the length of South Korea, which is similar in size. But it was taking far longer. There didn't seem to be any tunnels through the mountains—we had to go over or around them, adding hours to the journey. I remember seeing signs flash by—silver letters reading "Pyongyang," and the distance: 60 km, 30 km. . . . At last, I fell into an exhausted sleep.

When we finally arrived in Pyongyang at 7:30 A.M. on Saturday, March 21—the start of our fifth day in captivity—I was exhausted and disoriented. I didn't know what awaited me, but I knew it couldn't be good.

At those first military installations, the North Koreans hadn't seemed very well equipped to deal with us. The interpreter in Laura's interrogation wasn't very good. We had been able to destroy evidence, swallowing papers and damaging videotapes, and we had coordinated our stories despite the guards' efforts to stop us. Yes, they had gotten us to admit we worked for Current TV, and we had fingerprinted confessions. But apart from that, they hadn't gotten much.

Laura and I knew that Pyongyang would be different. They would have real interpreters, more-professional interrogators, and the technology and resources to find out things about us. Before we were separated, we managed to talk a little about how we should deal with the new interrogations that we feared were coming. We decided to put the responsibility on Mitch for what we had done—to tell them he had convinced us to do the story and that he knew more about the project than we did. This couldn't hurt Mitch, because he wasn't in North Korean custody, and it might help us—if we could stick to the plan. In facing more highly trained interrogators, though, we didn't know how hard this would be.

At long last, the car came to a stop next to a building. We all got out, and the officer who'd been sitting in the front passenger seat, whose name was Officer Lee, walked me inside. "You can get some rest now," he said.

Walking into the building, the first thing I saw was a very

large picture of a waterfall, painted on some kind of plexi-glass and lit from behind. We turned right at the picture and headed down a hallway, eventually coming to a door on the left side of the hall. Officer Lee showed me in, and I got my first look at the place where, unbeknownst to me, I would spend the next four and a half months.

There were two rooms—a bedroom adjoining a living room. But only the bedroom would be mine, as the living room was for the two female guards assigned to watch me.

I looked around in surprise—this place was much nicer than I had expected. There was a queen-size bed, a dresser, and a vanity with a mirror. And although it was decorated in that same 1980s-style decor, it was clean and comfortable. But the bathroom was the biggest surprise—it was big, with a black-and-white marble floor, white tiled walls, and a bathtub and shower. I had expected to be put in a dark room, like the cell at the military base, but this was like a hotel.

What did this mean? My mind raced. Maybe the North Koreans were planning to send me home after a simple paperwork process? If they were going to interrogate me, wouldn't they have put me in something more like a prison? I had been terrified of coming to Pyongyang, thinking that it meant I would be stuck in North Korea for a long time—but as I looked around this room, I dared to hope that might not be true. I wanted to somehow let Michael know I wasn't in a cell, that maybe I was going to be okay after all.

The room was chilly, and Officer Lee asked me if I was

cold. But I didn't want to ask him for anything. So I said, "No, I'm okay."

He gestured to a standing heater in the guards' room and said, "The heater may not cover your area, so you can use the electric blanket on your bed to keep warm." He seemed almost apologetic about the inconvenience, and I thought I saw a glimmer of kindness in his brown eyes. "Get some rest," he told me, and turned to leave. Alone in the bedroom, I sat on a corner of the bed and put my head on my knees, wrapping my arms around them. I felt like I should pray for something, but I was paralyzed. It seemed like my brain was frozen and had completely stopped working.

After Officer Lee left, the two female guards came into my bedroom. One was slightly older than the other, perhaps twenty-five to the younger guard's twenty-one or so, and both were tall and in good shape. The younger one had a sweet, open face, and the older one was pretty and spoke a little bit of English. They both wore their own clothes rather than uniforms.

They asked me what kind of food I liked to eat. "I don't like meat," I told them, "but I do like fish. But I'll eat anything, really." Later, I caught sight of one of them jotting something down in a ledger book, which I eventually realized was used to keep track of everything I said and did. The women seemed so nice, I felt even more hopeful that maybe things in Pyongyang wouldn't be so bad. And my hopes rose even more a short time later when breakfast arrived and they invited me into the living-room area to eat.

Emboldened by the guards' relaxed demeanor, I asked, "Do you know where my friend is?"

"I don't know," answered the older guard.

"She doesn't speak Korean," I went on. "She needs me to translate for her."

"Don't worry," she said, "they'll have a translator for her." She clearly didn't want to answer my questions, but I was desperate to learn what I could about Laura.

"She hurt her head," I said. "I'm worried about her. Can you find out if she's doing okay?"

"Don't worry," the guard said again. "They'll have medical care for her." She showed no signs of trying to find out anything for me, so I dropped the subject. But as I soon found out, I had already asked too many questions for Officer Lee's liking.

That afternoon, Officer Lee came back. He called me into the living room that adjoined my bedroom, and I walked in. For the first time, I took note of what was in that room. There was a big desk and chair, a TV, and a mustard-colored sofa with a coffee table. A large, wooden bookcase ran along one wall, and two portraits—one of Kim Il-sung and one of his son, the current "Dear Leader" Kim Jong-il—hung on another. The living room wasn't big, but it was clean and orderly.

Officer Lee appeared to be in his late forties or early fifties, very put together and professional, with neatly trimmed black hair and square gold-rimmed glasses. He was about five-eleven and in good physical shape, and his dark blue uniform was crisply pressed. On his collar he wore a badge with an image of Kim Il-sung.

He said, "Don't try to make small talk with the guards or ask them any questions. They are here to watch you, not be your friends."

A day or two later, Officer Lee began my interrogation. If at first he'd seemed like he was concerned for my well-being, now he seemed concerned with only one thing: getting information out of me. He asked my name, age, and religion. Right away, I wasn't sure how to respond. Should I tell him I'm a Christian? From my research, I knew that Christianity was banned in North Korea and that those who were caught practicing it were killed or sent to labor camps. I was afraid to tell him I was a Christian, as it would only add to the list of potential crimes I could be charged with. Yet I couldn't imagine denying my faith, either.

What should I do? I debated internally for what seemed like a long time, as Officer Lee waited silently for my response. I don't know where my courage came from, but I suddenly decided to tell him. "I'm a Christian," I said, and at that moment my fear melted away. To my surprise, Officer Lee didn't comment on my answer but just wrote it down.

He asked why we had been at the river, and I told him the same thing we had told the interrogators at the military base—that we were working for Current, making a documentary about doing business across borders. He looked at me warily, then abruptly left the room. It didn't seem like he believed me, but I hoped I would be able to stick to my story enough to convince him. I knew the interrogation process was just beginning, and I needed to be ready for whatever came next.

That evening, when the female guards brought me dinner, their demeanor had changed. They no longer spoke to me in a friendly, relaxed tone, instead just saying as little as possible, with stony looks on their faces. Once again I felt completely alone, and as I tried to eat the fish, rice, and vegetables on my plate, the tears started flowing. I couldn't stand the uncertainty—not knowing where Laura was, if she was okay, whether we'd get to see each other again, and what might happen to us. It was like a bad dream that just kept going on and on, no matter how badly I wanted to wake up.

❈

As bad as things seemed, they soon got worse. Officer Lee called me in to continue my interrogation, and the first question he asked was "Did you go to a church while you were in Seoul?"

I was stunned. How did he know? "No," I said nervously. "We didn't go to a church." I'm certain he'd seen the look on my face, but even if he didn't, he surely knew by the way I responded that I was lying.

As he had the day before, Officer Lee abruptly left the room. I sat there shaking, wondering how in the world he knew we had been to Pastor Chun's church. Had Laura told him? Or was he bluffing? Maybe he just threw the information out there, hoping I would confirm it? My head was still spinning when he stormed back into the room about ten minutes later.

"You didn't go to a church?" he yelled, his eyes furious. I stared at him, too frightened to respond. "Answer the question! A church where people were sitting on the floor, like a big living room?!"

"No," I said again, this time with even less confidence. "No, we didn't!"

Officer Lee wasn't a particularly big man—though he was tall for a North Korean—but he knew how to intimidate. He stepped toward me, rolling up his shirtsleeves like he was going to strike me. "You are *lying*!" he yelled, his voice so loud it filled the room. He kept yelling at me, cursing and shaking his fist at me, as I cowered in my chair. I burst into tears and jumped up, more scared than ever.

"I'm sorry!" I said. "We did go to the church."

"Think about what you did there!" Officer Lee barked, and left the room. Still crying, I went back into my bedroom. I knew he would ask me for all the details of what we did in Seoul, but how would I answer him? I didn't want to put anyone in jeopardy, but I was now in an impossible situation. How much did Officer Lee already know? I could just make up stories, but that wouldn't work—the North Koreans were interrogating Laura separately and would either know I was lying or think she was.

The next time Officer Lee came in, he wasted no time. He demanded details of whom we'd met with, and though I tried to give as little as possible, I told him we had met with a pastor. To my surprise, Officer Lee immediately responded with Pastor Chun's full name. The North Koreans obviously knew all about him and what he did—which meant we were in more trouble than ever. It meant they knew that the story we were working on for Current was about North Korean defectors.

Officer Lee began demanding all the details from our activities in Seoul. He would ask questions like "Who did you interview?" and "What did you ask them?" I tried to respond as vaguely as I could, but I also discovered something really strange: I couldn't remember most of the details. It was as if my memory was blocked, either from fear or some other subconscious impulse—I actually couldn't come up with details even if I tried.

When Officer Lee would ask a question, I would often respond with "I don't remember" or "I don't know." Sometimes, he would explode with anger and storm out of the room. When he came back, he would invariably have more details about our time in Seoul. He also knew other things, like the fact that Laura's sister, Lisa Ling, had once entered North Korea herself while doing a TV report about a Nepalese eye surgeon working there.

Was Laura revealing all these things? It seemed obvious that she was in the same building, being interrogated at the same time, and that Officer Lee must be going to that room to find out these details. It was like Officer Lee was in competition with Laura's interrogator, because whenever he got only small pieces of information from me, he'd say things like "You're not giving me anything! Laura is answering all of her questions!" Just as the other interrogators had done at the military base, they were trying to pit Laura and me against each other. And soon, it was working.

I felt frustrated, wondering why Laura would give up so much information—we had agreed to say as little as possible! And the more details Officer Lee told me, the more upset I got. I felt like I was in an impossible position, never knowing what exactly she was telling them or whether I would get in even more trouble for saying I didn't know anything.

Officer Lee would say, "Laura's confessing that her sister created a bad image of North Korea! You need to bring the level of your confession up to hers!" But I didn't know how to give him what he wanted. *I don't have a sister who's a famous journalist*, I thought. *I don't have a fancy title at work.* It felt like he wanted me to give him some kind of high-profile story or information, or show him that I was important back in the United States. But I couldn't.

He also wanted me to admit to committing a "premeditated, organized crime." He kept saying this phrase over and over, but I refused.

"There was no intent to harm your country!" I would say. But he had a ready answer.

"Did you show the beauty of North Korea?" he asked.

"No," I said.

"You see?" he replied. "It's a premeditated, organized crime to put our reputation down." According to North Korean law, it was illegal to defame the country. And because we were reporting about people who had fled North Korea and we had planned our trip in advance, we were therefore guilty in his eyes of committing a premeditated crime.

But those words scared me to death. I feared that if I allowed Officer Lee to bully me into saying them, the North Koreans might send me to prison for life, or even execute me. I was convinced that this was the phrase that would incriminate me forever, and I was determined not to say it.

Sometimes, Officer Lee would ask me about details that weren't true. Then I wondered whether Laura was making stuff up or the North Koreans were. Whenever these kinds of stories came up, I had a choice: Did I run with it, making up more false details? Or did I just say I didn't know what he was talking about? The interrogations were exhausting, as I was constantly trying to second-guess Officer Lee while figuring out how I could avoid revealing anything incriminating. But I also was trying to appease him, walking the fine line between giving details that wouldn't harm anyone and convincing him I was truly cooperating.

When Officer Lee finally left after the first day of interrogation, I felt broken. During those first four days of captivity, even when we were in prison cells and being interrogated, I had still somehow managed to feel like the detached journalist, trying to get the story. But now, after this bruising, frightening, angry interrogation, I realized deep down in my soul that I could lose everything that mattered to me—my family, my loved ones, my freedom. These people weren't messing around, and I was in very big trouble.

As I lay in my bed that night, I sobbed with anger—at myself, at the North Koreans, and at God. Where was He? Why had He deserted me in the hour of my greatest need?

I had always been a Christian, and I believed in God's goodness and that He watched over Michael, Hana, and me even in our most difficult times. Many times, I had turned to God in prayer, asking for His guidance, and most of the time I felt His warmth. But now all I felt was God's absence.

In all my life, no matter whether I was following God or not following Him, deep in my heart I always knew He was there. But whenever I didn't receive His help the way I wanted, or exactly when I asked for it, I complained like a rebellious child. Looking back, there was a reason for every decision God made, and often I would understand it later. But here, in this freezing cold room, miles from my family, with no idea when or if I would ever be set free, I felt He was failing to show me love. It was one of the most depressing and empty nights of my life.

I lay in bed, tears streaming down my face, and I thought obsessively of Michael and Hana. I felt I had failed them as a wife and mother—they trusted and loved me, and I had let them down.

Why had I been so stupid? Why had I taken the chances I did? Every time I pictured Hana's sweet face, my heart felt like it would shatter. I tried to imagine what she might be doing right at that moment: Walking to school with Michael? Sitting in her classroom among friends? Did she know I was in trouble? Did Michael? Did anyone?

❀

As I would later find out, Michael had learned about my capture at 5 A.M. Los Angeles time on March 17—which was 10 P.M. the same day in North Korea. While I was being interrogated at the military base, he was jolted awake at home by the sound of the phone ringing.

When he answered, groggy from sleep, he heard the voice of my Current colleague Adam Yamaguchi. Adam told him that Laura and I had been abducted and were being held in North Korea. He couldn't comprehend what he was hearing—he knew we hadn't planned to go into North Korea, so how could this be true? It took him a few minutes to understand what Adam was telling him, but soon he was wide awake.

Adam told him the basics: Laura and I had been captured at the border and Mitch had escaped. He said that Laura's family were aware of the situation, as he had called them three hours earlier. Apologetically, he told Michael that it had taken him three hours to track down our phone number, even though I had filled out an emergency-contact form for Current.

When Michael hung up the phone, he went straight to his computer to try to find any information he could. But there was nothing online—no one knew we had been captured except Mitch, Adam, our families, and a few other people at Current.

Next, Michael called the U.S. embassy in China to see if he could find out any information there. He called from our home phone, but no one answered. Twenty minutes later, he got a call on his cell phone from someone at the State Department in Washington. How they got his cell phone number so quickly after he'd called from home, he never found out.

"I was calling because my wife has been captured by the North Koreans," he told the person on the line, at the same time thinking how bizarre it was to be uttering such a statement.

"Yes, we've just gotten word," the person responded. "We're looking into it." They couldn't give him much information, but they promised to keep in touch with updates on our situation. He then called his mother to let her know what was going on, and contemplated what to do next.

Michael was scheduled to start a new temp job that morning, and despite everything that was happening, he decided to go ahead with it. He called to say he'd be fifteen minutes late but didn't say why. He also didn't explain why, all day long, he kept answering his cell phone—or that he was getting calls from the likes of Al Gore, who called that day to assure him that he would do everything he could to bring us home.

In fact, Michael didn't tell anyone else at work what was happening until that Friday, his fourth day on the job—regardless of the fact that every day he was taking calls from the State Department, heading out to his car so he could converse in private. Michael is a strong man, both physically and emotionally, and he was determined to shoulder the burden of what was happening and keep moving forward.

Five thousand miles away, I, too, had no choice but to keep moving forward, though with each passing day this felt harder and harder to do. Officer Lee had given me a pen and paper for the interrogation—he wanted me to write down details of our work in China and Seoul, to help me remember. But I found myself just staring at the paper, unable to come up with anything. Eventually, my thoughts would turn to Michael and Hana, and so I started writing letters to them. I poured out my thoughts and fears, even though I knew the letters would probably never be sent.

I wasn't supposed to use the paper for this purpose, and occasionally Officer Lee would reprimand me for it. But I didn't stop—it was one small way to feel connected to home. I drew pictures of Michael and Hana, little cartoon faces surrounded by hearts, always with big smiles. I wrote to Hana in Korean and Michael in English, telling him about what had happened and apologizing for having gotten into this situation.

On March 25, my fourth day in Pyongyang, I wrote to Michael:

I keep forgetting what day is today . . . I don't want to forget but I really have a short-term memory problem. I think today is Wednesday. Hmm . . . tomorrow is the day when I am supposed to come back to you. I am not sure how long the process will take here but I am just hoping that the DPRK [Democratic People's Republic of Korea] government will forgive me and have pity on me so I will see you guys soon.

A few hours later, after an interrogation session, my mood had changed:

I am worried now . . . I might not be able to go back home soon. I really did not want to make the officers here mad but I think I did.

I was overwhelmed with feelings of guilt, obsessed with how my detention was impacting Michael and Hana's lives. The next morning, after having an uncharacteristically good night's sleep, I felt terrible about it:

When I got up, I felt guilty that I slept well . . . You probably are worried about me so much and are not sleeping and eating well. I put you and my family in this hard time . . . I am so sorry. There is no word to express how much I feel sorry to you, Hana and my family. I miss you. I love you. Love you . . .

And soon enough, the guilt I felt extended to everything I'd ever done wrong to Michael, every way in which I had been a less than perfect wife:

> *I feel like I am always the one who doesn't support you . . . When I go back home, I promise that I will be a better wife. I will be a better mom. I will be a better supporter to you guys . . . I really miss you . . .*

Soon I was writing every day, page after page, to Michael and Hana. And when I wasn't thinking about them, I was wondering about Laura: How was she? Had the cut on her forehead healed? Was she scared? I wanted to ask the guards and Officer Lee, but he'd gotten angry when I asked too many questions before, and I was still afraid of him.

Officer Lee interrogated me every morning and most afternoons, with only Sundays off. He seemed to despise me, and his questions were often laced with sarcasm and anger. The kindness I thought I had seen in his eyes that first day was nowhere to be found. Instead, I saw a hatred that scared me.

The hours of interrogation were periods of nonstop stress, and at the end of each session, my underarms were soaked with sweat. I had never really sweated much before, especially when sitting still in a cold room. But those hours were nerve-racking, and invariably, by the time Officer Lee left for the day, I was a quivering mess.

I wanted to placate Officer Lee, but the only way to do that was by giving him information that could harm others. I tried every way I could think of to reveal things that would satisfy him without telling too much. I told him about going to the river on the morning of March 17—how we got there, what we did there, what we saw. But he always wanted more details. And I tied myself in knots trying not to give them to him.

Making my situation worse was the fact that I was still wearing the same clothes I had on when we were captured—brown corduroy pants and a white turtleneck sweater—and they hadn't been washed. The sweater had been a gift from my friend Su-yean during my short stay in Seoul, and I remembered the delight I'd felt when she'd given it to me just a week and a half earlier. Now, after sleeping in a jail cell and sweating through multiple interrogations, it was dingy and stained. At first, I had taken some comfort in wearing the sweater, but seeing it so damaged and dirty now made me sad.

There wasn't really any way to wash my clothes, as my room was freezing and even wearing everything I had—my pants, sweater, pajama pants, and the winter coat and some long underwear Officer Lee had given me—I was still cold. In fact, I never took off that coat during the first month except to sleep. Wearing the same unwashed clothes over and over, every day, was disheartening, as I'm sure my captors knew.

Not only was I cold, I had also gotten sick again. The whole first week in Pyongyang, I had terrible diarrhea, despite the fact that the food they were serving me actually wasn't too bad. My meals usually consisted of a piece of fish, some rice, and a couple of vegetable side dishes. I wanted to eat to keep my strength up, but almost right away I felt the familiar cramps and rumbling, and soon I was having trouble keeping anything in my system.

The North Koreans sent a doctor to check me out, and he said my diarrhea was due to the change in diet. He gave me a powdered medicine, but because of my burning-stomach experience at the motel, I was afraid to take it. "Do you know what opium is?" he asked me. "That's what this is. It can be used as medicine if you take it in very small amounts." I didn't want to take it, but when I told Officer Lee that, he yelled at me. "You will take it!" he said, and I had no choice but to comply.

In addition to being cold and sick, and wearing dirty clothes, I hadn't had a bath since our capture. Laura and I had been able to wash up a little bit at the last military base, but apart from that, I had managed only to wipe myself down a little bit with a washcloth and freezing water, as there was never any hot water in the bathroom here. Yet even though it was unpleasant, there was a part of me that didn't really want to have a bath. I was being held captive—it wasn't supposed to be a comfortable experience. In some ways, I feared that getting too comfortable would mean I was losing myself somehow.

So when my two female guards decided to prepare a hot bath for me at the end of my first week, I decided to wash only my hair, despite the effort it required for them to heat the water in the tub. First, they filled the tub with cold water, and then they put in an electric coil like a larger version of the kind used to heat hot water for tea. It took five hours to heat the water sufficiently, and the first time they did it, I had collapsed into sleep before the water was ready. They heated it again the next day, and I was able to at least feel the sensation of hot water again. I didn't know it, but this would be the first and last time I took a bath in this tub. It was too much trouble for the guards to heat all that water, so for the rest of my detention I ended up bathing in a very large stainless-steel bowl instead.

It felt good to have clean hair for the first time since I had been captured, and I was grateful to the guards for making the effort to heat the water. Amid all the uncertainty, every small kindness felt huge. Yet I was still overwhelmed by the hopelessness of my situation. I was absolutely alone, cut off from everyone I loved and everything I knew, with no idea when, or even if, my imprisonment might end.

But just as I was beginning to fear I had been forgotten entirely, my captors delivered an unexpected lifeline.

❈

It was the end of my first week in Pyongyang when Officer Lee brought in a business-size envelope for me. I had no idea what was inside, but when I tore the envelope open, my heart nearly leaped out of my chest. It was letters e-mailed from home!

My hands shook as I flipped through the e-mails, most of which were from my colleagues at Current. I hadn't been forgotten after all! The e-mails were filled with encouragement— comforting words from friends, telling me they knew Laura and I were here and that the government was working to get us home. I felt a tremendous flood of relief just knowing that we weren't alone and we might actually get out of this place.

In addition to the e-mails from my colleagues, there was a very short one from Michael. I could barely read it through my tears, but I read it over and over, even though it was only three lines long.

From: Michael Saldate
Sent: Thursday, March 26, 2009 3:50 A.M.
Subject: A letter to Euna

Dear Euna,
*   We love you and miss you. Please be strong and hang in there for us. We are thinking of you.*
*   Love,*
*   Michael and Hana*

I wondered why Michael's letter was so short when the others were longer and more detailed, but mostly I just felt a surge of love for my husband, who was at home thinking of me and praying for me while I languished in this strange place. I clutched the printed e-mail to my chest, hugging it like it was Michael himself, as the tears streamed down my face.

Officer Lee let me keep that e-mail from Michael, but he took the other ones back. Yet even though those letters are gone, I remember a few details from them. Adam Yamaguchi, my colleague who had called Michael to tell him we had been captured, wrote about a pair of yellow sneakers that I'd suggested he buy back in L.A. James Abee, who has a daughter about Hana's age, wrote that he and his wife understood how hard it must be for me to be away from Hana. And David Neuman wrote something that surprised me, saying that if I was reading his letter, I must have already met with "the Swedish ambassador."

I suddenly realized what Officer Lee had meant the day before when he asked me if I wanted to meet with the Swedish ambassador. I couldn't figure out why he would ask me such a thing, and thought he was just checking to see my reaction. It couldn't be true, could it? Why would the Swedish ambassador meet with me? So I simply didn't answer, unwilling to possibly make Officer Lee angry for something that would never happen anyway.

But when I saw David's note, I realized Officer Lee had really meant his question. He asked me again that day, with bitterness in his voice, "Do you want to meet with the Swedish ambassador?" This time, I said, "Okay." I also had another realization—that this was probably why they had allowed me to have a real bath, so I would look clean and well-treated when I met the ambassador.

At around 4:30 P.M. on March 30, nearly two weeks after we'd been captured at the river, Officer Lee came to my room and led me back down the hallway, past the waterfall picture, and outside for the first time in a week. The sun was blinding, and I could hardly believe I was able to smell trees, grass, and the outside world for the first time in so long. Officer Lee showed me into a waiting car—a Nissan sedan—and we set off through the streets of Pyongyang.

As we rode, Officer Lee said, "Look around. It's a nice area, isn't it?" He seemed to want to show me that Pyongyang, despite what I might have heard, was actually very pretty. And he was right. I eagerly took in the sights, looking out the car window for the entire ride. We rode to the Taedong River, which runs through the middle of Pyongyang, then across a bridge to Yanggakdo, an island that was home to our destination: the towering Yanggakdo International Hotel.

The Yanggakdo, one of North Korea's biggest tourist hotels, rises forty-seven stories into the sky, with no buildings nearby even close to it in height. It's an impressive sight, one of Pyongyang's best-known landmarks, and I stared up at it as Officer Lee walked me from the car into the building. He took me up to an empty third-floor meeting room, gestured to a chair, and said, "Wait here."

I sat waiting as Officer Lee bustled in and out over the next fifteen minutes or so. Finally, he came in and said, "Let's go." He took me to the next room over, and I walked in to see a tall, thin man in glasses waiting for us—the Swedish ambassador to the DPRK, Mats Foyer. His assistant was with him.

"Thank you so much for coming," I said, and we shook hands. Then he got down to business.

"We don't have much time," he said, "so I'm going to explain some things to you. You're aware of your situation, that there are no diplomatic ties between the United States and North Korea. I am here to represent you. Are you doing okay? Eating well?"

I told him I was, and I asked how Michael and Hana were doing. He said they were doing fine, then said he needed me to sign some paperwork. "This form gives me permission to release information about you. Who would you like the information to go to?"

I wasn't sure how to respond, so I said, "It's okay to share with my husband, family, and work, but I don't know who else would be good."

"Laura said it would be okay to share with individual members of Congress, work, and family, but not the media," he said. I could only assume this was because media interest had the potential to hurt the people we had been in contact with for our documentary.

"That sounds good," I said. "I trust Laura." So the ambassador filled in the information, and I signed the paper.

"Did you receive the package I delivered for you?" he asked me. "With the books, vitamins, and food?"

A day or two earlier, Officer Lee had told me he had a package for me, but he wouldn't give it to me. I didn't want to cause any trouble, though, so I just told Ambassador Foyer that I had received it.

"Do you need any more books?" he asked. He had brought me some novels in Korean, but he wanted to know if there was anything specific I wanted. I thought for a moment, then said, "Could I have *Jane Eyre*?"

"Charlotte Brontë's novel?" he asked. "I wish I had known, as I'm reading it now—I would have brought it for you." It felt so wonderful to have a connection with someone, and to be treated as an equal human rather than a prisoner and a criminal, that I felt myself tearing up again.

"Do you need anything else?" the ambassador asked.

I told him how much getting those first letters had meant to me and asked if I could receive more. I also asked whether I might be able to receive a new pair of pants, and perhaps some U.S. newspapers. He said he would look into it. And with that, it was time to go.

"I'll be back," he told me.

"Please come back," I said, desperate to see him again. We had been in the room together only ten minutes, and I couldn't believe it was already over and that I now had to go back to my guesthouse prison. Somewhat in shock and with tears in my eyes, I let Officer Lee lead me out of the room and back down to the car.

"Did that make you feel better?" he asked me.

"Yes," I said. "It did." After a moment, I asked him, "Is the U.S. government talking to your government?"

"Not yet," he said, looking out the car window. His voice was even, not like the angry, impatient voice he used in our interrogations, but this was the only information I would get from him today. The only other thing he said was, "When you talk with the ambassador, don't forget to ask him to help you. Don't just cry."

When we returned to the guesthouse, Officer Lee left me alone in my room; we wouldn't have any interrogation that day. Once again, I was overcome with emotion—sadness, frustration, fear, loneliness—and I cried until I thought my eyes would run dry. It was almost as if seeing a friendly face and getting letters from home reminded me of everything I was missing. The dreariness of my room and the uncertainty of my situation seemed even more impossible to endure. I read Michael's short letter over and over, clutching it until I finally fell asleep.

Six

ENDURANCE

THE NEXT MORNING marked two weeks since Laura and I had been captured. I hadn't seen Laura for ten days, ever since we were separated on the drive to Pyongyang. Every time I had asked to see her, I had been turned down. And it was clear from my conversations with Ambassador Foyer and Officer Lee the day before that we weren't going home anytime soon.

So when I woke up that morning, the only thing I knew was that I'd be facing more days with the same routine: eating, writing, and pacing alone in my room, and being interrogated by Officer Lee every morning and most afternoons. I hoped I would see Ambassador Foyer again soon, and that more letters were on the way, but there was no way to know for sure.

Those visits and letters were the only thing that brought me comfort in the first few weeks, as I couldn't feel the presence of God and wasn't strong enough to trust He was still there. It was only the things I could see—the letters from home, Ambassador Foyer's look of concern—that convinced me I wasn't completely alone.

There was little variation in my daily routine. I usually woke up around 7:30 A.M. The two female guards slept in the living room that adjoined my room, and if I heard either of them stir in the early-morning hours, the noise would wake me. Sometimes, I was lucky enough to have dreamed of Michael and Hana during the night, and I would cherish the vision of them and the feeling of being together, if only in my dreams. But no matter how real those dreams felt, I never woke up wondering where I was. As soon as I opened my eyes in that room, I knew I was still in North Korea, thousands of miles from my family.

I would wash my face and brush my teeth, and at 8, the guards brought me breakfast. Every day it was the same thing—rice, soup, and some vegetables. I always ate slowly, prolonging it as much as I could, because it was something to pass the time. At around 8:30, I'd finish breakfast and put my dishes outside the bedroom door. Then, from 8:30 to 10 A.M., I would either pace back and forth in my room or write letters to Michael and sometimes Hana.

At some point, Officer Lee implied it might be possible to send a letter home. I couldn't just write anything I wanted, though—I needed to make sure the letters were acceptable to the North Korean government. In fact, Officer Lee read drafts of a letter I was preparing for Michael, and he would give me suggestions for how to change it. That letter—the only one Michael ever received—went through multiple drafts before Officer Lee would allow it to be passed on.

I still have one of the early drafts of that letter, though it's different from what Michael ultimately got. Written on April 7, it gives an idea of what my early weeks in Pyongyang were like:

> *Dear Michael,*
>
> *It's Tuesday, April 7th, 2009. It's been almost a month since I left home . . . When I woke up this morning, I knew it would be a sunny day from the light coming through a curtain in my room. It reminded me of LA weather. I miss home . . .*
>
> *I am very thankful that the DPRK government allows me to write and to let you know how I am doing here. I am well treated here. The DPRK government is kindly taking care of me and I receive everything as needed. An officer gave me the email you sent me on March 26, and also showed me a letter to Laura from her sister because there was a mention of Hana in the letter . . .*
>
> *I miss you and Hana so much. Every morning, every night I think of you and Hana . . . I read the email you sent me every day . . . I'll keep myself healthy until I see you so please, please eat well, sleep well and take good care of yourself and Hana.*
>
> *I am sorry to put everything on you and am helpless here. I*

promise that I'll give you a break when I am back. I am just hop-
ing to come home soon . . .

You know the savings account that we didn't put your name
on? I hope you have access to it. If not, here is my permission.
I hope this letter is enough for you. I, Euna Lee, give permis-
sion to my husband, Michael Saldate to use (have access to) the
account. [signed] Euna Lee. There isn't much in the account but
I hope it will help you a bit.

Please discuss with Hana's teacher about kindergarten,
when to register and what you need to do. Again, I am sorry to
ask you so much . . .

Please tell Hana that Mommy misses her and loves her so
much . . .

In the beginning, I didn't write to Michael every day. But
later, after my interrogations were over, I wrote for hours on
end, filling pages with my thoughts, feelings, and fears. For
now, though, I'd write a few thoughts to Michael, or sometimes draw pictures of him and Hana, until Officer Lee arrived
for my morning interrogation. I also drew a calendar for
myself to tick off the days as they went by.

Every day except Sunday, Officer Lee would call me into
the living room for interrogation. And despite the fact that
he was aggressive and cold, provoking and manipulating me
psychologically, I actually found myself looking forward to
his arrival. He was my antagonist and my captor, but he was
an intelligent man whom I could at least have some kind of

meaningful interaction with. And he was sometimes the only person I spoke to—if it weren't for answering his questions, I might not speak at all for the entire day.

In the course of my interrogations, Officer Lee would bully, mock, threaten, and cajole to get the answers he was looking for. If I didn't give them, he would get angry and yell at me. These hours of questioning were exhausting, as I was constantly on guard. Officer Lee never tortured me, but he did play mind games intended to drive me to say things he wanted to hear. By the time we stopped for lunch, I was already emotionally and physically spent.

The guards brought lunch around 12:30, usually rice, a piece of fried fish, and vegetables. As with breakfast, I ate slowly, drawing what little pleasure I could out of the simple act of eating. Most days, after lunch, Officer Lee would come back for a second round of interrogations. Because these afternoon sessions might last for up to five hours, they were even more exhausting than the morning sessions.

Dinner came at 7:30 P.M., and I usually tried to go to sleep by 10 P.M. or so. The evening hours were hard, because I would think about Michael and Hana at home and wonder what they were doing. Lying in the dark in my room, alone for another night, I would pray to God for strength to get through the days until I might return home. Would He answer my prayers? At that point in my captivity, I wasn't sure He was even hearing them.

With the monotony of my daily life and the unrelenting

pressure of Officer Lee's interrogations, any change was welcome. And after seeing the Swedish ambassador on March 30, I got a particularly nice treat when Officer Lee passed along a bag of food items that the ambassador had brought for me. Inside, there was a bottle of orange juice, three cans of Coke, peanut butter, chocolate, Nutella, potato chips, and bread. Food from home! I was so excited! I drank the whole bottle of orange juice that day—I had been craving citrus and hadn't tasted anything so good in a long time.

But the care package came with a cost, too. When I told Officer Lee I wouldn't need any breakfast for the next couple of days, as I'd just eat the bread the Swedish ambassador had sent, he made a face. "You're going to eat that for breakfast?" he asked. He didn't seem to think bread could be a meal. Then, two days later, he instructed me not to eat any more of the food at all.

"Why not?" I asked. "It will just go to waste."

"Because we don't know what's in it," he replied. "We don't want to be responsible if you get sick or die."

I think he knew no such thing would happen, but his message was clear: If I continued eating the snacks, I would get in trouble. And he would know, because the guards made a note of absolutely everything I did.

Yet instead of taking the snacks away, he left them with me, which was a kind of torment. I did as he said, though, and stopped eating them—except for one item. I hid the peanut butter jar in my vanity drawer, underneath some clothes, and over the rest of my months in captivity, I would sneak a mouthful whenever I needed a boost. It was amazing how much comfort a tiny taste of peanut butter could bring me.

❖

During those first few weeks in Pyongyang, when I had tried to hear God's voice and feel His presence, I couldn't feel anything. Whenever I didn't know how to answer a question during an interrogation, I would ask God to guide me. I would ask for signs, hoping to hear His voice for what to say to protect myself and people we interviewed. But the irony was, as desperately as I sought His guidance, I didn't have the strength or patience to hear His answers.

This was a very dark time. No matter how hard I tried or how much I prayed, I just couldn't get past the feeling of being alone.

In early April, as I was walking back into my room after an interrogation session, I was surprised when a gospel song I hadn't thought of in years suddenly poured out of my mouth. Based on the Prayer of St. Francis, the lyrics say, "Lord, make me an instrument of your peace. Where there is hatred grown, let me sow your love. Where there is injury, Lord, let forgiveness be my sword. Lord, make me an instrument of your peace."

At first, I just sang, taking comfort in the melody—but when I realized what the words said, I panicked. What did this mean? I didn't want the Lord to use me for peace! I didn't want to be an instrument—I just wanted to be home with my husband and daughter. It felt like God, by sending this song to me, was asking me to do something I wasn't prepared to do. I tried to push the song out of my head, frightened by what it implied. What if God's plan for me meant I would have to stay in North Korea for a long time?

This wasn't the message I wanted to hear. I needed something concrete to hold on to, and just a few days later, I got it.

About a week and a half after I met with the Swedish ambassador, Officer Lee brought me a second batch of e-mail. I was so excited to have more news from home—and this time, there was a long news-filled letter from Michael. My hands were shaking as I read quickly down the page.

> *Euna,*
>
> *Sorry for the first letter being so short, I didn't have much time to put it together. The State Department didn't tell me when I could write until the courier left, so I wrote something really quickly. Now I just want to tell you the latest here and to remind you how cute Hana is . . .*

I smiled at these words, and the tears spilled again. As I read through the letter, I was relieved to see that Michael and Hana seemed to be holding up well, and that friends and family were looking out for them. Michael wrote that he was talking with my sisters Jina and Mina every day, and that his father had come to visit, as well as our friend Aaron. But the details I cherished most were about Hana.

> We had improv rehearsal at the house the first week, and Hana wouldn't go to sleep as she wanted to join us. She was so cute and she had so much fun, because here we were a bunch of adults basically playing, and she ran around and jumped . . . Hana was in one [scene], jumping around me, saying, "Daddy! Daddy!" And then a girl in our group played Hana in the second scene. It was so funny, and Hana laughed. She said, "Is that me?" I said, "Yes," and she laughed.
>
> Oh, I almost forgot to tell you that somebody got 100 per-cent on her final spelling test. She did really well. I was so proud of her. She got the princess prize because she did so well . . .
>
> Honey, I want you to hang in there. Hana and I are fine, so just hang in there and be patient. Hana and I love you so much and I don't have the words to express how much I love you and miss you . . .

Reading these words was like a balm to my soul. I had been so worried about Michael and Hana, but it sounded like family and friends had rallied around them and they were try-ing to go on with life as usual. Reading Michael's words, I was able to picture Hana jumping around with his improv group, delighted to be included. It was a tremendous relief to think of her happy and carefree at home.

Having this letter in my possession was like having a secret treasure. It gave me strength when I felt down and reminded me that despite the situation I'd gotten myself into, Michael still loved me. I had felt so alone in those first few weeks, but this letter was proof that I wasn't really alone at all.

And not only was Michael thinking of me, so were many others—my sisters, my mother and father, my colleagues and friends all sent letters, which I read eagerly, over and over. Some sent news: My friend Christof wrote about his trip to Italy; another friend wrote about Captain Sullenberger landing his plane on the Hudson River; Laura's aunt, whom I had never met, wrote about Somali pirates in the news. I was touched that all these people took time out of their days to write to me, and happy to have something other than my own situation to think about.

And there were letters that made me laugh. My friend Benita sent riddles, hoping to entertain me in case I had nothing to read. She also sent a funny letter with the results she got when she Googled the phrase "make the time pass in isolation." These were some of the suggestions she found, and she added her own commentary:

> *Blink wildly and then close your eyes really tight for an interesting light show (Amusement Potential: 1–5 minutes) . . .*
>
> *Try not to think about penguins (Amusement Potential: 1–5 minutes). This is especially hard, because by trying too much, you remember what you were trying to avoid thinking of. If you try too little, you end up thinking about penguins anyway.*

Pretend you're a robot (Amusement Potential: 1–3 min-
utes). Walk down the street with mechanical movements, adding
"zzzzzt" sounds with each motion . . .

I laughed out loud reading Benita's letter—one of the few times I laughed during all those months in North Korea. Another time was when I read my older sister Mina's descrip-tion of her son getting braces:

My son put braces on his teeth. As you know, his teeth were really
ugly. When he laughed or smiled, he looked like Dracula, didn't
he? But after wearing braces, another problem comes out. What
is it? I will tell you. Now he looks like Frankenstein when he
opens his mouth, which is much worse.

I laughed so hard when I read this, as I could just imag-ine my nephew's look, but it also crushed my heart. My sister Mina is a serious person, not one to joke—especially about her children. She was obviously trying very hard to cheer me up, and it touched my heart. Reading these words made me miss her all the more.

The greatest gifts in the letters, though, were the Bible verses and inspirational thoughts my friends and family sent. During those first few weeks, when I was feeling the absence of God so painfully and lived in fear of Officer Lee's wrath, I felt more alone than I ever had. I was so obsessed with the situation at hand—interrogations and the conditions of my captivity—that I forgot about the broader promises that God makes, to hear our prayers and never give us burdens greater than we can bear. I was incapable of seeing beyond the four walls I was trapped in until a dear friend named Nzingha sent me a letter with words that knocked those walls down.

Friends and family had been afraid to send Bible verses to me, as they were afraid the North Koreans would refuse to pass the letters along to me. But Nzingha forged right ahead. In one of the darkest periods of my interrogation, at a moment when I was paralyzed with fear, I received a letter from her with comforting words of the Twenty-third Psalm: "Yea, though I walk through the valley of the shadow of death, I will fear no evil, for thou art with me." From then on, whenever I felt fear, I would cling to the words of this verse. It felt like God was telling me directly that He was with Michael, Hana, and me through everything.

I also drew strength from letters sent by people I didn't even know personally. Ann Song, whom I had never met, sent me song lyrics and verses, and one in particular really helped me. She sent me a quote from 2 Corinthians that reads: "So we fix our eyes not on what is seen, but on what is unseen. For what is seen is temporary, but what is unseen is eternal." Reading this verse, I realized that I had been putting all my faith in what I could see—the letters, the time I spent with Ambassador Foyer—but I was forgetting about that which is unseen: God. From the time I read that verse, I tried to remember.

I was so happy to be hearing from everyone, and relieved that people hadn't forgotten about Laura and me. Throughout my first month and a half in Pyongyang, I received letters every ten days or so, and then I got them even more frequently. And that wasn't all. Sometime in mid-April, Officer Lee gave me two printed-out photographs from home. The first was of Hana on a swing, gazing up at the sky with a beautiful, hopeful smile on her face. She's wearing her pink Puma shirt, which she calls her tiger shirt, and a gray denim skirt, and she looks as though she's longing for something fantastic, far off in the distance.

I realized that this was a photo from the church picnic we had attended—the same church picnic where I had been so distracted by thoughts of work! It seemed so long ago, I couldn't have imagined it had happened just a week before my trip. I could remember how patiently Hana had waited for her turn on the swing, and how proud I was of how she shared with the other kids that day. Seeing her happy smile again, and remembering how much I had let my work get in the way of our relationship, I couldn't stop the tears from streaming down my face.

The second photo was of the three of us—Michael, Hana, and me—on our ninth wedding anniversary the summer before. Michael and I were dropping off Hana at a friend's house before going out to dinner, and the friend snapped a quick photo. The three of us have our arms around each other, and we all have the most contented smiles on our faces.

I stared at those two photographs until I had every detail memorized, and every day I would pray while holding my family's hands, asking the Lord Jesus to bring us back together as a family. All I could think was, *I want to get back to that life. I want to get back to Michael and Hana.* The photos gave me hope and reminded me what I needed to be strong for. Because as difficult as these first four weeks had been, things were destined to get worse.

❀

Throughout April, my interrogations with Officer Lee became even more intense. Every session, he seemed to know more about what Laura, Mitch, and I had been doing and whom we had met. And he would use that knowledge to try to goad me into revealing even more information.

It was a cat-and-mouse game. I told him generally about the farmer's wife and Young, the Internet sex worker, but I made sure to leave out any details that could be used to identify them. I never revealed names, and I knew Laura wouldn't either, as they were Korean and therefore foreign-sounding to her. In fact, the one time Officer Lee said a name that was supposedly one of the defectors we had met, it didn't even sound like a Korean name. I assumed it must be Laura's closest phonetic guess, but when Officer Lee asked me about it, I just said, "I don't know. I never asked for names."

Every time I said, "I don't know," it enraged Officer Lee.

He continued to pit Laura and me against each other, saying things like "She's telling us all the details! You're not telling us anything!" He also tried to turn me against her by saying things like "Laura says she didn't understand anything in Korean, and that you were in charge. She said *you* know everything, not her." It didn't occur to me that this might just be his technique to break me down, and unfortunately, it began having the effect he wanted. I found myself getting more and more frustrated with Laura. Why was she telling everything? Was she really blaming me for everything?

"Laura said you seemed very close to Pastor Chun," Officer Lee taunted. "She said you two were laughing and talking, and that you didn't translate anything for her." He also said that everything that was happening was our own fault. "*You* went to the border on the seventeenth. *You* brought this on yourself. You have no one else to blame." This played on my already crushing sense of guilt, and I felt angry at Laura and myself, rather than at the North Koreans who had abducted us and were holding us prisoner.

No matter what I told Officer Lee, he constantly pushed for more. He repeatedly accused me of holding things back, and called me a liar when I said I couldn't remember details. Every day was an agony of trying to decide what I could safely reveal, knowing that he could erupt at any moment.

One strategy was to play dumb. At the end of an interrogation session, Officer Lee would sometimes give me a specific subject to think about for the next time. Then, if he asked about anything else at the next session, I would try not to give any details at all. "You told me to think about this other subject," I would say, "so that's all I've been thinking about. I didn't know you wanted anything else."

I also spoke very softly with him, in a low monotone. "Speak up!" he would say, but I never did. I wanted him to think I was weak, both physically and mentally, because then he would be less likely to torture or hit me.

For days, I debated whether I should reveal that the guide and I had gone alone to the Tumen River on the night before our capture. Maybe, I thought, this would satisfy Officer Lee's need to know more while not harming anyone else. But was it really so harmless? Was there some way he could use that information against the guide? Or against me? The more I thought about it, the more confused I felt. I was scared and had no one to turn to for counsel. Around and around I went, agonizing as I tried to make what felt like life-or-death decisions.

Finally, one afternoon I blurted it out. "I didn't tell you this earlier, but the guide and I went to the river the night before," I said. "We wanted to shoot some footage at the border." My heart was pounding in my chest, and I held my breath as I waited for Officer Lee to respond.

"Okay," he said without interest. And that was it. All that agonizing I'd done was for nothing—he didn't seem to care in the least. What was important and what wasn't? What was dangerous for me to reveal? I realized I had absolutely no idea, and it made me feel even more off balance and uncertain.

Another tactic Officer Lee used was raising questions about the motives of Pastor Chun. He knew about the videos we had watched with the defectors in Seoul, and even described the video of the two young men scaling the fence to seek refuge at the German school.

"Think about it," he said. "Who is filming these kids? Don't you think that, by showing them in a video, someone is putting them in danger?" He let his words sink in, then went on. "Did those boys make their 'escape' by choice? Or were they used?" It had never occurred to me that Pastor Chun might be putting defectors in danger for his own purposes, but was that in fact what he was doing?

"What you don't see on that video," Officer Lee went on, "is that there were five boys! Three of them didn't make it and were arrested, but they left that part out!"

Officer Lee's words sent a chill through me. What did I really know about Pastor Chun, anyway? The more Officer Lee implied that Pastor Chun was in this for himself, the more confused I felt. Was Pastor Chun sacrificing people for his cause? Was he reckless, or was he a hero? I felt sick as I thought about how we'd taken everything Pastor Chun said at his word, having been in such a hurry to get everything done during our short time in Seoul and China. Maybe Officer Lee was right—maybe Pastor Chun had just been using us. Sitting in that interrogation room, shut off from the rest of the world, anything—even worst-case scenarios—felt possible.

Officer Lee knew he was getting to me, so he turned the heat up even more. One morning in late April, he burst into the room already yelling. "You had a meeting about this 'project' with your boss and lawyer at work!" he yelled. "This was planned out! It was a *premeditated crime!*"

His rage scared me, and I cowered in my chair. "I'm sorry! I'm sorry!" I pleaded, but he wasn't finished. He started shouting the names of people at Current—the head of programming, the legal counsel. It was shocking, and frightening, to hear him yell out the names of my colleagues and recount the discussions we'd had, and I started to panic. I slid out of my chair and onto the floor, curling up in a ball. I wanted to cry out, to beg him for forgiveness, but my mouth was so dry with fear that nothing came out.

"Someone will be responsible for this crime!" he shouted. "And it's going to be you!"

Then he spoke the words that would haunt me. "You think about your daughter," he hissed at me. "Think about whether you want to go home or not."

At that moment, I realized suddenly that in trying to protect everyone—the defectors, Pastor Chun, Laura, and even myself—I had neglected to protect the most important person in the world to me: my daughter. I hadn't thought about what I needed to do to get home to her, and now Officer Lee was implying I might not make it if I didn't cooperate. Once again, as I seemed to do so often, I had thought about others' needs before those of my family. Why did I take them so much for granted? I had always assumed that I could give them help or love whenever I wanted—whenever it suited *me*.

As I lay on the floor, crying, I felt a hollowness in my soul. I was really·stuck—no matter what I chose to do, someone was going to get hurt. What could I do?

"Say it!" Officer Lee yelled down at me. "Say it was a pre-meditated crime! You planned this, and you must confess!"

I couldn't say those words, but I did blurt out something else. "I think I'm pregnant!" I wailed, fearing my words would enrage him more.

But at that moment, Officer Lee wasn't angry. He seemed stunned.

❀

Michael and I had been trying to have another child, and when I skipped my period in April, I thought for sure I was pregnant. I had intended to wait to see whether I would miss another period, but I was terrified at the turn this interrogation was taking—afraid that the stress and fear I felt in the face of Officer Lee's rage might harm the baby I thought I was carrying. Before I knew what I was doing, the words were out.

Officer Lee stood silently as I continued. "I didn't want to tell you," I said, afraid to look at him. "I wanted to wait another month—to be sure." I was afraid of the consequences if it turned out I wasn't really pregnant. But I had acted instinctively to protect the baby I believed was inside me. When he was yelling at me so furiously, all my strength had drained from my arms and legs, and I had to sit down. I couldn't look at him, but I knew he was still angry.

"So what if you're pregnant?" he snapped. "You can still go to prison. We have doctors in prisons!"

He stood looking down at me, then said with disgust, "I don't believe anything that comes out of your mouth." And that was the end of our interrogation for the day.

In my unsent letters to Michael, I told him about what happened, but not about the clash with Officer Lee:

April 23

Honey,

I feel very weak today . . . no energy . . . Guess what? I might be pregnant. I skipped my period this month . . . I am very happy and at the same time I thought what a bad time to be pregnant, when you are not next to me to take care of me . . . I love you and Hana . . . I gave you guys a kiss on the picture that you sent me this morning . . .

April 25

Michael,

It's very quiet today . . . I saw the officer this morning. He brought me new shoes and a spring jacket. I felt really bad to receive them. I didn't feel I deserve them . . . I gave my urine to the officer for the pregnancy test. I am just waiting for the result . . .

April 26

Honey,

The officer said the result of the pregnancy test was negative. So I am not pregnant. I guess it's a good thing . . .

I was disappointed when Officer Lee told me the test results, although it was hard to imagine enduring this detainment while being pregnant, too. I had so many complicated feelings about it—I wanted so badly for Michael and me to have another child, and for Hana to have the little brother or sister she wanted. And if I was pregnant, then surely I would make it home before giving birth, as Michael had seen in his dream. Yet I couldn't imagine being pregnant while thousands of miles away from them. My feelings were jumbled, veering from disappointment to relief.

Somewhat to my surprise, I found that my feelings were just as mixed about Officer Lee and the North Koreans in general. Despite the psychological torment of Officer Lee's interrogations, and despite all his threats and shouting, I began to believe that, at heart, he was actually a good man. That may seem a strange thing to say about one's captor, but I really did feel that way.

In the same April 26 letter I wrote to Michael to say that I wasn't pregnant, I also wrote this:

The officer is really nice. I respect him a lot. I wish I wasn't here for the investigation. I have to say the people in DPRK are really nice. They are just people like us.

And it was true—I did respect Officer Lee. I knew that when he interrogated me, even harshly, he was doing his job. But at other times he showed flashes of the kindness I thought I'd seen in his eyes that first day in Pyongyang—kindness that seemed genuine.

For one thing, he was very nice to the two female guards, acting in an almost fatherly way to them. He joked with them and brought books from his home for them to read. He also was supportive of the older guard's desire to study English, even asking me if she could have one of my books when I was finished with it. And when he found out that Hana and I spoke Korean with each other, he made no attempt to hide his delight that I was teaching her the language of her heritage.

Officer Lee was also a gentleman. He never walked into my room without asking or at least making a sound to let me know he was coming. And he performed occasional small acts of kindness, like bringing me fruit juice, or a branch with acacia flowers from outside after I'd told him I loved the scent of acacia. Once, he even propped open the heavy curtain in my room, which was always supposed to be shut. He'd seen me sitting on the floor in the one spot where a narrow sunbeam peeked through a crack in the curtains, so he put a chair by the curtain to hold it back, allowing more sun into the room.

With very few exceptions, the other North Koreans I met seemed to be good people, too. Despite the fact that I was a presumed criminal, nearly everyone showed me kindness, even though they were under orders not to interact with me.

The kindnesses may have been small, but they felt big to me. One day, one of the guards had gone out for a while, and when she returned she offered me a handful of cherries she'd picked from trees behind the guesthouse. Another time, I told the younger guard that I liked a certain song I'd heard on the TV they had in their room. From then on, she would turn up the volume for me whenever that song came on. And another woman, who was apparently the building manager, always had a smile on her face when she stopped by. Though I didn't learn her name, I nicknamed her "Sunshine."

The guards weren't supposed to have conversations with me, but over time they became less strict about following that rule. One day, I asked to borrow some nail clippers. I wasn't allowed to take them into my room, so I sat and clipped my nails while the guards chatted. They were talking about Korean popcorn—a sweetish puffed corn snack—and I told them that when I was younger, you could buy it from street vendors.

"You'd bring your own cone," I said, "and the guy would fill it up. Do you have that?"

The guards got excited. "Yes!" one exclaimed. "I love popcorn!"

At that moment, it was easy to see us all as simply Koreans rather than as people on opposite sides of the ideological divide. Food in particular had a way of doing that, as it reminded me that we all shared a culinary heritage. Sometimes while in Pyongyang I found small rocks in my rice, and these brought back particularly vivid memories. I remembered, as a child in South Korea, washing the rice to make sure the tiny rocks were rinsed out. It had been years since I'd seen rocks in a rice bowl, but as soon as I saw them during my detainment, I was transported right back to my childhood in Seoul.

The guards were very businesslike with me, but they were still young—not much older than girls, really. Living full-time in the room next to me, with only short breaks, had to be difficult for them. Sometimes the older one would go home to get clothes, but the younger one wore the same thing almost all the time. To sleep, they took turns on the couch. The older one would stay up late, watching me or reading books, while the younger one slept. The older one was always looking out for her, like a sister, and she would teach her English phrases with a pocket conversation book.

The younger one would sometimes pass the time singing songs. She had a beautiful, clear voice, but when she sang songs in English, her pronunciation was terrible. She particularly liked one she'd just learned—"My Heart Will Go On," the Celine Dion song that was the theme of the movie *Titanic*. One day, as I listened to her singing it in the next room, I wrote down the lyrics. Much later, I told her, "I can teach you better pronunciation. We'll act like I'm not talking to you, but I'll say the words so you can hear." And every once in a while, she would ask me what something in English meant—but only when the older guard wasn't nearby.

Each guard would have the occasional conversation with me, but only if the other wasn't around. One day, when the younger guard was away, the older one told me about how sorry she felt for South Koreans. "When we were in high school," she said, "we cried for South Korean kids who have to ask for money on the streets. We would see pictures of them in school."

"What are you talking about?" I said. "South Korea is strong economically, so most kids don't have to beg."

She looked shocked. "Well, some do," she said. And she was right, of course. Just as I had felt sorry for North Korean children, the people in the DPRK pitied South Korean kids. But did either truly know what was going on in the other's country?

I came to understand that, for the most part, we know only what our own countries tell us about others. When I began hearing what the North Korean government said about the United States, I understood why people call us "coyotes"— the North Korean news portrayed us as tricky and mercenary. The guards turned on their TV every evening at about 5 P.M., and whenever something came on about America or South Korea, they would turn up the volume to force me to listen.

The first show was always news, which was invariably filled with critical commentary about South Korea and the United States. But the programs that really showed the depth of North Korean contempt for America were the documentaries.

Mostly about the Korean War, these documentaries portrayed American soldiers not just as the enemy but as bloodthirsty, evil murderers. Older North Koreans, interviewed on-screen, described terrible crimes committed by American troops—scenes of stabbing, rapes, and even baby killings. Witness after witness told graphic stories of the Americans' terrible cruelty, and after a while it started to get to me. Were we really as bad as these documentaries claimed? Did the Americans cover up their own atrocities? Who was telling the truth?

The documentaries were the worst, but nearly every show on North Korean television took aim at the United States in some way—even standup comedy and kids' shows. I was shocked to see one children's show in which an older man was teaching children how to read: Instead of reading aloud fairy tales or adventure stories, he read from a book that described American atrocities in the war.

It was incredibly stressful to listen to these stories, and once I even stuffed toilet paper in my ears, trying to drown out the sound. It was no wonder Officer Lee hated me and wanted to see me sent away to prison! If he believed everything he was taught, it was a wonder he didn't want to see me dead.

Yet Officer Lee continued to show small kindnesses to me as well, in spite of everything. The day he was so furious about the meeting at Current TV—the day I told him I thought I was pregnant—he came back in the afternoon with an envelope. "I almost ripped this up, I was so angry," he snapped.

"Just remember that I was nice and generous enough to give it to you."

Inside the envelope were photos of Hana. I wept when I saw them, and said, "Thank you, Officer Lee." Perhaps he gave them to me as psychological bait, to jolt me into confessing more details so I could see Hana again. Perhaps everything he did was to manipulate me into doing what he wanted. But it didn't feel that way. It felt like he had given me a gift, and I was grateful.

At the end of April, the interrogations began to slow down. For six weeks, Officer Lee had pushed me to my limits, but now his attitude seemed to be changing. The questioning became less intense—it was more about getting straight the details he already had, rather than pushing for new details. I was relieved that things seemed to be calming down, but wary, too. The next step would be a trial, and I didn't want to have to go to a courtroom to face charges.

On May 1, the International Workers' Day holiday, Officer Lee said, "There will be fireworks tonight. Do you want to see them?" I honestly didn't care about seeing fireworks and would have preferred to stay in my room. But he seemed to want to show me, so I said, "Okay."

At around 8 P.M., he took me up to a second-floor balcony along with two guards. The fireworks were beautiful—giant colored flowers exploding against the night sky—and it was really nice to be out in the fresh air. We watched for about fifteen minutes, and then Officer Lee brought me back to the room. He began telling me about a book he thought I would like: Kim Jong-il's writings on the art of the cinema.

"It's a beautiful book," he said. "When you go home, I'll give you that book as a gift."

I didn't believe that would happen anytime soon, so I just smiled. But as I learned later, the North Korean and U.S. governments had planned to open up talks around that time, so Officer Lee must have believed Laura and I might really be going home soon. Those talks fell through, however, so Officer Lee began preparing for the next phase: writing up a confession, based on my interrogations, that I would sign before going to trial.

It was as if Officer Lee and I were entering a truce of sorts, though I knew our battle was not over. And just a few days later, everything exploded again.

❈

One morning in early May, Officer Lee walked into my room holding Laura's notebook. So many weeks had passed that I had forgotten about it entirely. But seeing it in his hands sent a fresh jolt of fear through me, and I could tell from his face that he was furious.

"What is this?" he asked me, his voice on edge.

"It's Laura's notebook," I said, looking down at the floor.

He leaned in close. "Where did you learn how to eat paper?" he asked.

How does he know? I said nothing, but my whole body shook. How could this be happening? Our interrogation was over! And now this?

"You ate the paper, huh?" he said, laughing derisively. "And threw away your phones and tapes? Did you think we wouldn't find out?" My mouth was so dry, I couldn't speak. I said nothing, but he continued to bait me.

"You know I have tried to help you, but you are poking your own eyes out! You are responsible for this," he said, waving the notebook at me.

What should I do? He already knew what I had done, but should I deny it? Was he guessing, or did he know for sure? How should I respond?

Officer Lee kept berating me, and he went in and out of the room, as if to collect more information. Each time he came in, he pushed me harder, trying to get me to admit what we had done. Finally, my heart racing, I blurted, "We both ate the paper!" I said. "She ate half and I ate half!"

But Officer Lee had a ready answer. "Laura says she has an ulcer so she couldn't eat it," he sneered. "*You* ate it all. *You* are the guilty one."

I will confess that at that moment I hated Laura. With the benefit of hindsight, I realize that both of us revealed things under duress, and that Laura might not even have said all the things Officer Lee claimed she did. But the North Koreans were very good at turning us against each other. These were not amateur interrogators, like the ones at the military bases near the border; the interrogators here in Pyongyang knew what they were doing, and they did it very well.

To this day, Laura and I have never discussed what we told our respective interrogators. But I know she did her best to protect me and everyone else. Laura and I endured an experience that has bonded us together forever, and I respect her and consider her a good friend. At the time, however, I felt angry and betrayed. And I thought Officer Lee really meant what he was saying—that Laura would get to go home and I would have to stay.

And Officer Lee wasn't finished with me yet. A little while later, he brought in the videotapes we'd had when we were caught. He put them down—six in all—and said to me, "I know which ones you damaged, but I'm going to give you the chance to tell me yourself."

My heart sank. He knew everything! This was my worst nightmare, even more frightening than being told I was betraying my Korean blood. With the tapes and the notebook pages, Officer Lee knew I had tried to sabotage their investigation. And he was furious.

Reluctantly, I started examining the tapes. I could tell which were the damaged ones because the ribbons had been pulled back into the cassettes after I split them. I handed those two to Officer Lee, and he nodded. I knew he would have them fixed, and I feared what was on them.

A couple of days later, he walked into my room with transcriptions of the two videotapes. He began reading excerpts to me, and I realized with horror that he was quoting the former officer I had interviewed my last day in China. I had intended to digitally alter his voice once we got back to the United States, but of course I hadn't been able to do that. Now the North Koreans had a tape with his voice on it, saying things that were considered treasonous.

I felt sick. We had promised to protect the people we interviewed, but now the tapes were in the hands of the North Korean authorities. I felt especially upset about the officer—he had been so nervous about the interview, and I had convinced him we would protect him. We had wanted to do a good thing, to shine a light on the darkness of the defectors' situation. But now we were potentially harming the very people we wanted to help, no matter how hard we had tried not to.

Officer Lee taunted me, parroting back my own words on the tape. I had told the officer about watching *Seoul Train* a few years earlier, and I said that bringing the story of North Korean defectors to light felt like a personal mission to me, not just professional. I had told him it felt like God's calling.

"You think that's God's calling?" Officer Lee spat at me. "You think God sent you?" His voice dripped with sarcasm. "So you think you're some kind of prophet?"

Officer Lee seemed disgusted by the fact that I was a Christian and I believed God was working in my life. "You didn't do this as God's calling," he said. "You did this to make a name for yourself at work. To make more money." I didn't answer, but I was frightened. Would I now be charged with spreading Christianity in addition to the other charges? In North Korea, this was a crime that could add even more years to my possible prison time.

At that moment, I couldn't breathe or speak. I felt paralyzed by the thought that I might never see my beautiful daughter again. Even worse, I feared that her last memory of me would be a terrible one—that she would remember only that night before I left, when she wanted to help me with the photo album and I simply ignored her. The guilt I felt about that incident was almost unbearable, and there was nothing I could do to fix it.

On May 2, I wrote to Michael:

Honey, [Hana's] voice has been in my ears . . . her asking me, "Why aren't you giving me any more pictures to help you?" is in my ears, and every time I hear her voice, it hurts me so much. It hurts me . . .

I am hoping she will forgive me. I am hoping that that isn't the last thing she will remember of me. Please, please give me one more chance to go back to her. And one more chance to be a good mommy to Hana. One more chance to be a good wife and a good person.

I was obsessed with the idea that I needed to be a better person, that I had been following the wrong priorities for too long. Why had I been so focused on my career instead of my family? How had I gotten so off track? I made lists of things I would do differently when—or if—I made it home. I promised myself that I would be a more attentive mother and a more loving wife.

But there was nothing I could do now, and every time Michael sent news of Hana, it tore at my heart. In late April, he'd written that she'd had photos taken for her preschool graduation. She had dressed in a white collared shirt for the occasion, and I was devastated that I couldn't be there to help her get dressed and fix her hair. She needed her mom, and I wasn't there. I was letting her down.

Looking at pictures of Hana gave me strength, but it also crushed me to know I couldn't touch her. Being apart from her was so painful, it felt as though my heart might explode. I had to find a way to connect somehow with her, even though we were five thousand miles apart.

So I began a new ritual. Every day at 1 P.M. North Korea time, I'd stop whatever I was doing. Back home in Los Angeles, it was Hana's bedtime, 9 P.M. Hana loves princesses of all kinds, but her favorite story had always been "Sleeping Beauty." I had read her the story so many times that I could recite it by heart—and so I did. I told the story aloud as if Hana were right beside me. I even pretended I was carrying her, holding a pillow as I would a baby. The guards might have thought I was crazy, but these actions calmed me. For those fifteen minutes each day, I felt a connection with Hana.

I also made a strange discovery when I was trying to figure

out which story to recite for Hana. I considered "The Little Mermaid" and "Cinderella," but when I went through those stories in my head, they had something disturbing in common: The main characters had no mothers. As it turns out, that's true for many other beloved children's stories, too, such as "Bambi" and "Finding Nemo." I had never realized this before, but now I found it incredibly upsetting. Where were the mothers? So I stuck to "Sleeping Beauty" and tried to put those other stories out of my head.

❖

Throughout the first two weeks of May, the interrogations again slowed to a crawl. Officer Lee now spent most of his time working to craft a confession for me that was similar to the one Laura's interrogator was preparing for her.

He didn't question me anymore, but he would come in with papers, reading things aloud to me and asking, "This is what you said, right?" By now, I didn't care anymore what he was asking—I just said whatever I thought would make him happy. If he had something wrong and I told him that, I knew he would be angry. And I didn't want to face his anger anymore.

But there were times when I couldn't escape it. Officer Lee had built up a competition between Laura and me, and as he pulled together my confession, he couldn't resist taunting me some more. He told me he believed Laura more than he believed me, and he made fun of me for trying to protect her. "You're so naïve," he said. "You think you're protecting Laura. But you're just criminals! One criminal trying to protect another!"

Technically, I wrote my own confession, but it was really Officer Lee who wrote it. I had to think of how to write things properly in Korean, so he would tell me the phrases to use. After a while, I'd just ask, "What do I say next?" and he would tell me. It was a very detailed confession, based on the notes Officer Lee had taken during my dozens of hours of interrogation.

As hard as I'd tried to keep from revealing any damaging information, Officer Lee had broken me down, pulling details out of me that I wish I had been strong enough to conceal. I had admitted that Pastor Chun was involved in our project, that we'd met with North Korean defectors, and that we were doing a documentary about them—all things that Laura and I had hoped to keep secret. While writing my confession, I felt a fresh wave of guilt about everything that had taken place. How had this happened? How had everything gone so wrong?

On May 14, Officer Lee presented me with a twenty-seven-page confession. With tears streaming down my face, I put my fingerprint on it—terrified that by doing so I was sealing my fate, consigning myself to years in a labor camp. But I didn't feel I had a choice. It was clear now that we were definitely going to trial, and Officer Lee had told me all along that if that happened, we would receive a long sentence. With a sense of despair, I realized that my fate was sealed unless the U.S. government intervened. Where were they? Was anyone going to help us?

The same day, I got at least a partial answer when I learned that I would be seeing the Swedish ambassador for the second time. "You've got to beg this guy to help you," Officer Lee said. "Don't just sit there calmly! Tell him you need his help, to get yourself sent home!"

I had been in shock the first time I met with Ambassador Foyer, but this time, facing the possibility of years in prison, I didn't need Officer Lee to goad me into showing some emotion. I was a wreck. We made the drive to the Yanggakdo International Hotel, and as soon as I saw Ambassador Foyer in the same third-floor conference room, I burst into tears.

"Please, help me!" I begged. "I'm a U.S. citizen—they have to help me! They can't leave me here!"

"Your government is working hard, Euna," he said, his face filled with concern.

"You say that," I cried, "but why is there no news from the U.S.? Why isn't anything happening?" I began wailing, and the ambassador got up and moved to the chair next to me. He put his arm around me and squeezed my shoulders.

"We're working on it," he said again, his voice gentle.

But his words did little to calm me. "Please," I said, raising my voice louder than it had been during my entire time in North Korea. "I have a daughter! She needs me! She's only four!"

For about five to ten minutes, we went back and forth—me crying and begging, and Ambassador Foyer trying to soothe me. He kept saying they were working on it, but what did that mean? Where was the proof? I felt like I had waited patiently but, now that the DPRK had my signed confession, I might get sent away forever.

"I don't want to go to prison," I cried. "I can't be separated from my family for that long! If I go to prison here, you'll lose contact with me!"

"We never will," he said, continuing to squeeze my shoulders.

"Please don't tell Michael I cried this much," I said.

"Don't worry," he said. "This is normal."

With that, a North Korean officer interrupted. "That's it," he said. "Time to go."

I spoke softly to Ambassador Foyer so that only he could hear me. "I don't want to go," I said. "I hate to leave this room!" He just looked at me, his eyes filled with concern. I couldn't stand the thought of going back to the guesthouse, of once again being alone with my thoughts and fears and guilt.

"I'll try to visit you again," he said, his eyes filled with kindness. "Just remember, don't look too far in advance. Take one day at a time."

"Please visit me again," I said. "Please . . ." But the guards were already leading me out of the room.

Back in the car, I was still shaking and crying. But Officer Lee turned to me and said, "You did a great job!"

I remembered what he'd told me before my meeting, and I realized he thought I'd done all of that for show, to convince Ambassador Foyer to help me. For a moment, I thought, *He's crazy*. I didn't answer him, just wept quietly all the way back to the guesthouse.

Seven

OUR DAY IN COURT

T HE OPENING OF MY TRIAL was set for Thursday, June 4, 2009—three weeks after I fingerprinted my confession. Now that Officer Lee was no longer interrogating me, there was little for me to do except wait and worry. I paced back and forth in my room for hours on end and continued to write notes—most of which would never be sent—to Michael, my parents, my sisters, my friends and colleagues. And every once in a while, Officer Lee would give me letters or photos from home.

Off and on, I asked Officer Lee whether there was any news about my situation from the United States, as he seemed to have access to either international TV or the Internet. He almost always said no, but one day in May, he told me that

Michael had gone to Washington, D.C., to meet with Secretary of State Hillary Rodham Clinton. "She promised she's going to help out," he told me. My hopes soared. At last, someone was listening—someone who might actually be able to bring us home!

After that, whenever Officer Lee showed up, my heart would jump—was he coming to tell me I was being released? I desperately hoped that we would be set free before the trial, and I sensed that Officer Lee did, too. He often urged me to impress upon Ambassador Foyer, Michael, and my colleagues that Laura and I might receive long-term imprisonment if the trial went forward. He always told me to beg for the U.S. government's help; it was almost as if the North Koreans were hoping the United States would reach out first.

I was relieved to hear that Secretary Clinton was on the case. Now that the highest levels of the U.S. government were involved, surely they could figure out a way to get us home while still saving face for North Korea? But the days passed, and Officer Lee brought no more news from home. And toward the end of May, he asked me, "Do you want a lawyer to represent you at your trial?"

I hadn't considered this, and it seemed odd. Who could defend me? It didn't seem like anyone could effectively argue my side. I thought for a moment, then said, "Could you do it?" Admittedly, because Officer Lee was my interrogator and had taken my confession, it wouldn't make much sense to have him represent me. But I believed he had a good heart, he seemed to have a certain degree of sympathy for me—and besides, I had nothing to lose by asking. My mother had written to me that if I could plead my case to one person and move his heart, that person might help me. I believed Officer Lee could be that person.

Officer Lee laughed. "I'm not a lawyer," he said. "You can hire someone to represent you in the trial, but you will have to pay them." Even though the DPRK was a socialist country, he explained, I didn't have the right to free legal representation.

I thought about it, but ultimately I decided there was no way a North Korean lawyer could possibly defend my interests. The DPRK government was too punitive—surely, anyone who actually defended me well would get into trouble for it. So, given that a lawyer probably wouldn't be effective and I'd have to pay for it, I decided I wouldn't have one. *God will defend me*, I thought. *I will put my faith in Him.* I would pray for God to speak through me, to soften the hearts of the prosecutor and judges.

The closer we got to the trial, though, the more nervous I became. By the end of May, I had been in captivity in North Korea for more than two months. I had gotten over the initial shock of being held prisoner and had adjusted somewhat to the rhythm of life at the guesthouse. But being detained in a Pyongyang guesthouse was one thing—getting sent to prison was something else entirely. I knew that Laura and I would be found guilty at the trial, and I was terrified that we would be sent immediately to a remote prison, never to be heard from again.

As thoughts of prison swirled through my head, I couldn't

stop thinking of Michael and Hana. I missed them so much, it felt as though my soul was tearing in two. The emotion kept building up until the evening of May 26, when it burst out in a relentless flood.

I wrote to my friend Mariana about it in a letter composed the next morning, May 27:

> *My days here are very simple and my emotions are pretty unstable, as you can guess. I crashed out last night, crying so loud . . . I usually sob so I don't bother anyone, but I did not care last night. Just looking at my Hana's picture, I could not help myself. Mariana, there is no word that can express how much I miss my baby and Michael. These are the reasons I hold myself strong, and at the same time I get crushed . . .*
>
> *I can't forgive myself whenever I think about what I did to my family, but I hope I will have a chance to make up this time for them . . .*

Then, just when I feared I couldn't take it anymore, my captors threw me another lifeline.

❈

Officer Lee had told me there was a possibility I would be able to call home before the trial, and on May 27, the same day I wrote to Mariana, he came in and said, "We will let you make a call to one family member."

I was overjoyed, but also afraid my hopes, now raised so high, could be brutally dashed to pieces. "I want to call my husband," I said. "But what if he doesn't answer the phone?"

"You can call someone else," he said.

Then it hit me—did I even know anyone else's number? Whenever I called people at home in L.A., I relied on the contact list on my cell phone. I never bothered to memorize their numbers. It was even harder to remember as almost two months had passed since I'd called anyone at all.

I started writing down random phone numbers on a piece of paper. After trying more than twenty times, I finally managed to remember the phone number for my younger sister, Jina, who lives in San Francisco. I also wrote Michael's cell phone number down several times to make sure I had it right. This was my one chance to communicate with my family, and I had to make absolutely sure I got through to someone.

Officer Lee led me outside the building, and once again we got into a Nissan sedan and made the drive to the Yanggakdo International Hotel. I was taken to conference room number 5 on the third floor, where a beige phone sat at the end of a long table. It was about 2 P.M. on a Wednesday afternoon, which meant it was 10 P.M. Tuesday in Los Angeles.

"You have ten minutes," said Officer Lee.

I punched Michael's number into the phone, my hands shaking. It rang once, twice, three times . . . and then went to voice mail. I immediately hung up, afraid that was the only chance they would give me.

"Can I call him again?" I asked, my heart frozen with fear.

"Yes," Officer Lee said. And so I punched in Michael's number again. And again, the phone rang several times, then went to voice mail.

"You have to call someone else," Officer Lee said.

"Let me call once more," I said, frustrated. "I'll leave him a message this time." Officer Lee nodded, and I called Michael one more time. When his voice mail clicked in, I left him a message. I don't remember exactly what I said, but I told him not to be angry with himself for missing the call, as I knew he would be. And I told him I was going to call my sister Jina, so he could find out from her what was happening. I was crushed at not being able to talk with him, but there was nothing I could do.

I dialed Jina's number. "Jina, it's me—your sister!" Just saying those words made me choke up with emotion, but when she uncertainly replied, "Sister?" the tears began streaming down my cheeks.

Fortunately, Jina was calm, which settled me down quickly. I only had ten minutes, so we had to get right to business.

I told her I was being treated well and was healthy. She told me that Michael and Hana were fine, and that Hana had been accepted into a Korean/English program for kindergarteners. She also said that my mother was flying to L.A. from Seoul to attend Hana's preschool graduation on June 26. I felt grateful to my mother, but devastated at the thought that I might not be there myself.

"I want to be there for Hana!" I said, the tears coming again. "I want to come home!" I told Jina that Laura and I were being sent to trial and would be sentenced to a long prison term unless the United States intervened.

"Don't worry," my sister told me. "Be strong, you'll be fine. Stay positive and keep yourself healthy. You'll be coming home soon."

All too soon, Officer Lee pointed to his watch as a signal that it was time to hang up. Reluctantly, I told Jina I had to go and said I loved her. "Thank you for looking after Michael and Hana," I said, and she replied, "No need to thank me." Jina had lived with us for the first three years of Hana's life, and the two of them shared a special bond. I felt fortunate to have her helping Michael with looking after Hana.

As I hung up the phone, I was overcome with emotion. What a relief it was to hear my sister's sweet voice—but what a bitter disappointment not to be able to talk to Michael.

I sobbed as Officer Lee walked me out of the room, and as we passed through the hotel's lobby to get back to the car, he said, "Wipe your eyes! Pull yourself together!" He didn't want anyone to see us and wonder who I was, but I was beyond caring. I was pierced through with grief. Talking to Jina had felt like a final confirmation of my situation: I was a prisoner in North Korea, a place where no one in my family could reach me. And being so close to talking with my husband, but then being denied, was almost worse than never having had the chance at all.

I cried all the way back to the guesthouse, but after I got into my room and reflected on my conversation with Jina, I realized something. Perhaps it had been God's plan that I would end up talking to Jina rather than Michael. After all, she was able to talk with me calmly and tell me about how things were going at home, whereas Michael and I probably would have been overcome with emotion. And she had told me Michael was doing a great job with Hana, which put my soul at ease.

A couple of hours later, I became even more convinced this had been God's plan when Officer Lee came back into the room and asked me, "Do you want to talk to your husband?"

"Yes!" I said, sitting bolt upright on the bed.

"Let's go," he said. He walked me out to the car and we went back to the hotel. I could hardly believe it, I was so excited. Even though I had told myself it was better to talk to Jina first, I had been incredibly disappointed—but now the best possibility was coming true: I would get to talk with Michael *and* Jina, instead of only one of them. And it was only possible because Michael missed my calls the first time around.

By now, it was the middle of the night in Los Angeles, but when I dialed, Michael picked up after one ring.

I can't even describe what a relief it was to hear my husband's voice. He immediately started apologizing for missing my calls earlier, but I said, "It's okay, it's okay! Don't worry!" We were hardly able to talk about anything substantive, as we both were crying and saying "I love you!" over and over. It was wonderful to talk to him, but it also made me very emotional, as I could hear the uncharacteristic depression in his voice.

I wanted so badly to talk to Hana, too, but she was sleeping and I feared it would be too disruptive—and confusing—to have Michael wake her. What would she think, hearing my disembodied voice in the middle of the night after all these weeks? She would want to know when I was coming home, and we had no answer to that question. No, it was better to let her sleep, no matter how much I wanted to talk to her.

"Please take care of Hana," I told Michael. "Tell her I love her!" He promised he would. Once again, Officer Lee began tapping his watch. I couldn't stand to end the call, and I just kept saying things like "I love you" and "I'm doing fine" and "Please take care of yourself," until finally I had to put the phone down.

As Michael would tell me later, he'd been at Bible study that evening and had put his phone on vibrate, so he hadn't heard the first three calls. When he heard my message later, he was incredibly upset and angry at himself—he couldn't believe that he'd missed our one chance to talk to each other.

Laura's sister Lisa Ling, Michael, and Laura's husband, Iain, had become close, talking to each other every day during our detainment, so Michael called Lisa right away to ask if she'd gotten a call from Laura. Lisa said she had, and apparently, after hearing the pain in Michael's voice, she called her mother and told her about it. Mary Ling then went into action, calling someone in the State Department to report that Michael had missed my call to him. The State Department got in touch with Ambassador Foyer, who then contacted the North Koreans to say, "Please let Euna try again." And mercifully, wonderfully, they had allowed it.

As soon as I got back to my room, I wrote Michael a note:

Honey,

I just talked with you on the phone. Is this real? I was so happy to hear your voice . . . I wish I could fly to you right now and be with you. I will be strong as I promised you. I will be strong. I often forget but I'll try, because I love you so much. I'll wait patiently and be positive. Oh . . . it was so good to hear your voice. Honey, don't stay up now, go to bed, okay? Get some sleep for tomorrow. I love you so much . . .

❖

On Monday, June 1, three days before the trial started, I was allowed to see Ambassador Foyer for the third time. I was much calmer than I had been the last time, and I told him I'd been receiving the letters and photos from home, as well as some care package items—eye drops to treat a chronic problem I had with dry eyes, a few shirts, and some books. We talked a little bit about what might happen during the trial and afterward, and he told me the North Korean government would not allow him to attend the trial.

"They say it's for your protection and privacy," he said. "They're not allowing any foreigners in the courtroom."

I was disappointed but not really surprised. Officer Lee and his colleagues didn't seem eager to have the trial on display, and they knew they couldn't stop foreign observers from releasing information about it. So they simply refused to let them observe.

Ambassador Foyer could tell how nervous I was, so he offered me some words of encouragement. "Don't think of the trial as only a negative thing," he said. "It might serve to open up a conversation between the two countries." I looked at him skeptically, but his face was sincere. He seemed to believe this might be true, so I took some comfort in that.

The next day, June 2, Officer Lee gave me a few more letters. One of them, from Laura's husband, Iain, included photos of Hana taken at their house in L.A. when she and Michael were visiting. Hana looked so big! But her hair had grown long and hadn't been combed, her dress seemed wrinkled, and she had a serious look on her face. All I could think was, *Hana needs her mother at home*. It was painful, but I couldn't stop looking at her.

As hard as it was to see Hana's photo, Iain's letter gave me great strength thanks to a particular line that really resonated with me. "Please do not give up hope," he wrote. "Think of every day as the start of the journey home, one less day away from Michael and Hana." I had been thinking of every day as one *more* day away from my family, with each day feeling harder than the next. This line touched me and gave me hope. I would think of it often during the trial and afterward.

I was very calm the last few days leading up to the trial, but when I woke up on June 4, I could feel a knot in my stomach. I wondered whether I had made a mistake in declining the help of a lawyer, and suddenly I realized I'd be standing alone in front of not only the judges who would decide my fate but a professional prosecutor who might interrogate me even more harshly than Officer Lee had.

All morning, I sat nervously in my room, waiting to be taken to court. Officer Lee had told me what clothes to wear: a pair of brown canvas pants, a light pink button-down shirt, and sneakers—all of which he had brought me when the weather had turned warmer. He also told me to pull my hair back tightly into a ponytail.

I sat on my bed, waiting, and eventually two female soldiers walked into my room. They were very strict, not like the guards who normally watched over me. "Get up," one barked. "Stand over here. Put your hands out like this." I put out my hands, and she handcuffed me. Officer Lee had warned me that I would be treated like a criminal, but I had forgotten how humiliating that feeling was. I started to cry.

The two soldiers walked me outside to a waiting minivan, put me in the back seat, and got in themselves, one on either side of me. "Put your head down," one of them ordered, and I did. We drove around for twenty minutes or so and arrived at the court building. As we got out of the van I wanted to see where we were, but the guard barked again, "Put your head down." They led me into the building and up to a third-floor waiting room. After a short wait, they led me into the courtroom.

The chamber was old, with off-white walls and cracks in its concrete floor, and it didn't look like a Western courtroom. There was a desk with three chairs for the judges, who sat in the front of the room on a raised platform, and a chair and desk for the stenographer. Observers, including the female soldiers who had escorted me to the courthouse, sat on long pews facing the judges. On the right side of the room was a desk for Laura's lawyer, and on the left was a desk for the prosecutor. In front of the first pew were two chairs—one for Laura and one for me.

This would be my first time seeing Laura in two and a half months. In that whole time, I had never stopped asking Officer Lee if I could see her, and there were many days when I desperately wished we could communicate. But when I finally saw her, I had an unexpected reaction. I felt completely removed from her emotionally.

All those days of interrogation—of hearing that Laura was supposedly cooperating more, or telling her interrogators I was responsible for everything, or revealing things we had agreed to keep secret—had hardened my heart toward her. She may not actually have done any of those things, but Officer Lee had done such a good job of pitting us against each other, I didn't even want to look at her when she walked in.

Though we sat in chairs right next to each other, I just put my head down. Both of us were crying, but at that moment we were of no comfort to each other at all.

A bailiff opened the proceedings and the judges and prosecutor came in. The first thing they asked us was, "Look around. Is there anyone in the courtroom that you don't want here?" Laura and I both said no. And then the prosecutor asked me to come to the stand. I nervously walked to the front of the room.

His questions were simple; he asked me to say my name and list my family members. I sat down, and then it was Laura's turn. The prosecutor asked her the same questions. To my surprise, as soon as she began answering, the hardness in my heart just melted away. How comforting it was to hear her voice! I kept my head bowed, not looking at her, but as I heard her speak on the stand, I could feel myself begin to relax. I wanted her to keep speaking, just to hear her voice, but the prosecutor asked her to return to her chair.

The prosecutor then read aloud both of our confessions, Laura's in Korean and then English, and mine in Korean. Someone said, "This trial is open"—and then asked Laura to leave the room. We would be tried separately.

I wasn't supposed to look at Laura, but out of the corner of my eye I could see her as she stood and walked out. She was wearing the same brown canvas pants as I was, and a similar shirt but in white instead of pink. Her hair had grown so long since we'd last seen each other! It was tied in a ponytail with one of the two handkerchiefs that had been used to blindfold us all those weeks ago, and she held the other handkerchief in her hand.

When Laura was gone, I took a deep breath. It was time. I sent up silent prayers to God: *Please control my tongue. Don't let me say anything stupid. Please give me a piercing voice to touch these judges' hearts so they'll have compassion.*

I took the stand, and the prosecutor began asking me some very strange questions. He brought up a South Korean woman named Im Soo-kyoung, who had famously traveled illegally into North Korea in 1989 to go to a youth festival, and asked if I knew her. I was in high school at the time and had heard about her in the news, but I answered truthfully that I didn't know much of anything else about her. He also asked me about the pastor who had gone to North Korea to bring her back, but I didn't know anything about him except his name.

The first part of my testimony went on like this, with the prosecutor asking questions that were unrelated to my own case. This seemed strange, but I just kept answering the questions, hoping I was making a good showing. Eventually, though, the prosecutor got around to asking specific questions about me. At that point, things heated up.

He asked me why I had gone to South Korea and China on this trip. I answered that I had watched the movie *Seoul Train*, and said that I felt compassion for the people who were in it and wanted to help. As soon as the words were out of my mouth, I could see that they had infuriated the prosecutor and the judges.

"Help?" the prosecutor shouted. "Help what? The criminals who have broken our laws?!" He began railing at me, accusing me of trying to harm the DPRK. "You have Korean blood!" he yelled. "Why are you betraying the Korean people?"

"I'm sorry!" I answered, frightened by his outburst. "If I had ever met a North Korean in my life, I would have thought differently about your country. I don't hate North Korea!" I tried to placate the prosecutor, but it was too late. I was so upset with myself—why had I answered the question in that way? I should have known it would make them angry.

The prosecutor's outburst threw me off, and for the rest of the questioning I stumbled through my answers. I couldn't keep things straight, and I veered off into tangents that made the prosecutor and judges even angrier. "Just answer the question!" the prosecutor would bark, and I would struggle to find the right words to satisfy him. It felt like I was going around and around, and I knew I was doing a terrible job of representing myself.

I wanted to show them that, although I'd grown up in a different ideological system, the documentary was meant to help people, not create a bad image of North Korea. But the more I tried to do that, the worse things got.

Mercifully, the first day of the trial finally ended. Officer Lee, who had been waiting in a room next door, met me outside the courtroom when the two female soldiers brought me out. We all got into the minivan and rode in silence. After a while, I noticed that the drive back seemed to be taking longer than the drive there, and because I wasn't allowed to look out the window, I suddenly realized I had no idea where we were going. Were Laura and I going to be put into prison while we were on trial? I sat silently, my heart pounding, until the minivan finally stopped and I was let out. To my relief, we were back at the guesthouse after all.

Officer Lee walked me back to my room and asked the guards to bring me some strawberry juice. It seemed like he was the one person who was looking out for me, and with my emotions in such a jumble, I actually felt guilty for putting him in this position. He could tell I was upset, and he asked, "Are you okay? Were you scared?"

"Yes, I was scared," I said. "The prosecutor asked so many questions, and he got angry at my responses!"

"Well, he's a prosecutor," he said. "He's doing his job." He tried to calm me down, but I couldn't relax. He stayed with me for about twenty minutes, then left. But an hour and a half later, at about 6 P.M., he came back.

"You know what?" he said, "Laura's doing a great job at her trial. She's even saying, 'I forgot to tell you this in my interrogation,' and is confessing more. Why aren't you doing that?"

Yet again, he was pitting me against Laura. "Don't compare me to her," I said bitterly.

"Just speak clearly," he said. "That's all you have to do."

"I'm not a reporter!" I snapped. "I'm an editor, I work behind the camera! Stop comparing us!"

But Officer Lee wouldn't give up. He walked me through some important questions I would be asked and told me what I should say. My emotions were all over the place—guilt, frustration, fear, anger. I just wanted to be alone in my room, to decompress after this difficult day. Finally, he left, and I lay awake for a long time, unable to sleep.

The next morning, June 5, I was still on edge. I wrote a terse note to Michael:

I was so naïve and stupid. Not intelligent enough. Not logical enough at the trial yesterday. All my thoughts were scrambled in my head and tumbled . . . They didn't come out right through my mouth. This morning, I was thinking, "Why didn't I answer this way or that way?" Too late to bring up the right answers . . .

Oh, I hope the judge will forgive me . . . I feel so weak, I feel so stupid . . . I need your wisdom, honey. You always gave me good advice when I am confused, when I am stressed . . . I really hope I won't be so stupid like yesterday . . .

❈

Later that morning, the same two female soldiers took me back for the second day of my trial. In the waiting room beforehand, an officer came in and called my name. I stood up, but he said, "Sit down. Don't be scared." I sat back down.

"If you don't understand a question in the courtroom, ask what it means," he said. "Answer slowly." It was obvious that everyone—the judges, the prosecutor, Officer Lee—was unhappy with my testimony. I thanked the officer and made a silent vow to do better today.

The good thing was, I had been here once before and knew what to expect, so I was less nervous. But as soon as the proceedings started, things changed. The main judge thought the prosecutor wasn't doing a good enough job, so he started asking me questions himself. And he got right to the heart of everything, asking me directly about the defectors I had met, Pastor Chun, and the documentary we were making. Just as I'd done during the interrogation with Officer Lee, I tried to walk a fine line, giving the judge answers that satisfied him without going outside the bounds of my confession.

Sometimes, when I answered questions in a way the judge didn't like, he'd just interrupt me and change the subject, apparently because they didn't want certain things going into the court record. I tried to explain that, because I grew up in South Korea, I may have a different ideology, but that didn't mean I hate North Korea. I told him I had been taught from a very young age that North Koreans were the enemy.

"When we played jump rope," I told him, "we would sing a song that was all about defeating North Korea—" But he cut me off, uninterested in hearing the rest. The judge made it very obvious when he was happy with an answer and when he was not, and I found myself trying hard to please him.

To my dismay, the prosecutor played the tapes of my interviews with the former North Korean officer we had met in China. I felt sick hearing his voice, remembering how nervous he had been about protecting his identity. Damaging the tape hadn't worked, and the very thing he feared had come true—the North Koreans had his statements on tape.

Not only was the videotape used as evidence against me, but it also seemed to make the prosecutor angry for another reason. On the video, as I interviewed the former officer, my voice was strong and clear, and my questions were articulate. The whole time I had been in North Korea, I had spoken softly and frequently answered "I don't know" during interrogations. Compared to my demeanor on the video, it was like I was two different people. When Officer Lee had first seen the tape, he had said, "Why don't you answer questions like that? Why are you playing dumb?" And the prosecutor and judge seemed to feel the same way.

At one point, the judge asked me a question I didn't expect. "About your documentary," he said. "How did you think it would benefit the U.S.?"

I didn't think it would benefit the United States at all, but should I say that? It would certainly benefit Current TV if it did well, but was that an appropriate answer? All I could think was, *What did Laura say?* I knew I needed to say something—to give them what they wanted to hear—but I just stood there silently, my thoughts going around and around, for about ten seconds. And suddenly, I remembered something Officer Lee had accused me of doing early on in my interrogation. Perhaps this was the answer the judge was looking for?

I decided it was worth finding out. "Well," I said, "maybe the documentary would help the U.S. if it isolates your country from the world."

As soon as the words were out of my mouth, the judge slammed his fist on his desk, making me jump. "Isolate us?" he yelled. "What are you going to accomplish by doing that?" He hit his desk again, clearly enraged.

"You are worse than Laura!" he continued, his voice booming off the walls. "You are betraying your own blood! You are a *betrayer!*"

I burst into tears, scared out of my wits. I knew that the word "betrayer" was a loaded term in the DPRK; I had read that people who were labeled "betrayers" by the government were often given the death penalty. A thought suddenly flashed into my head: *I am going to die here.*

The judge went on, his anger intensifying. "To me, and to this nation, you are a betrayer!" he yelled. "You have ruined the reputations of people whose same blood runs through your veins!" He was irate, lecturing me at the top of his voice. "You are Korean and have betrayed your Korean blood! Your crime is much worse than Laura's, and you will be punished for it!"

The rest of that day in the courtroom is just a blur in my memory. Deep in my soul, I believed that I had just been given a death sentence, and I was as scared as I had ever been.

What had I done? What would happen to Hana—how would she live without a mother? How in the world had things gotten to this point? I couldn't even grasp what was happening anymore; the only thing I could think was, *They're going to kill me. They're going to kill me.*

I cried all the way back in the minivan, as Officer Lee sat stone-faced in the front. He said nothing to me the whole way, but as soon as I got back into my room, I knew I had to talk to him. I was crying so hard I could barely get any words out, and the guard seemed shocked at the state I was in. "Can I see Officer Lee, please?" I asked, my voice breaking. She left to get him.

When Officer Lee walked in, he said, "What's wrong?"

"I cannot die here!" I cried. "The judge told me I am a betrayer, which means I'm getting the death penalty! You have to help me!"

"Follow me," he said, and abruptly turned to leave the room. I followed him down the hallway, and he took me outside, where no one else could hear our conversation.

"Listen to me," he said, turning to face me. "You are not going to die here. Why would we make your four-year-old child motherless?"

I wanted to believe him, but I couldn't. I was paralyzed with fear.

"You say that, but you're not the judge," I said.

"Under our laws, we don't kill foreigners," he said. "It's not how we do things."

"You're not the judge," I said again, convinced that the judge, by his choice of words, had made clear what fate awaited me.

Officer Lee leaned closer. "Have I ever lied to you?" he asked. I shook my head. "No? Then trust me. You need to trust me. You will not die here."

I looked into his eyes and saw the same glimmer of warmth I'd seen my first day in Pyongyang. Much later, I realized that Officer Lee probably wasn't supposed to try to comfort me, which is why he wanted to do it in private. I don't know this for sure, but I believe he was too compassionate to watch me suffer, so he bent the rules to reassure me. It's one of the many moments during my captivity when he showed me compassion—and one of the reasons why, even though he was my interrogator and captor, I remember him as a good person.

Officer Lee's words did comfort me. But I was still fearful—and now I would have to wait the entire weekend before court reconvened on Monday, June 8.

❁

Over the weekend, I was a wreck. Officer Lee would come to check on me, but most of the time I was just sitting on my bed with my arms wrapped around my knees, dreading what was to come. I knew we would be found guilty, and I was sick with fear about what the sentence might be.

On Monday, June 8, the female soldiers loaded me into

the minivan for the third and final time. When they took me to the waiting room at the court building, there were female doctors there. I thought, *They're here in case I faint or have a break-down*, and just the thought of it made me extremely nervous. I sat with my head down, rocking back and forth in my chair. I couldn't breathe, and my whole body felt ill.

"Why don't you go to the bathroom?" Officer Lee said. I didn't really need to go, but I did as he said. A soldier escorted me to the first-floor bathroom, and when we got back, Officer Lee leaned close to tell me something.

"You're not going to get the death penalty, okay?" he said. "So don't panic."

I nodded, but it was impossible not to worry. For the next half hour, I just kept rocking back and forth in my chair, nearly hyperventilating. Finally, it was time to go into the courtroom.

The judge asked me only one question: "Do you have anything to say to this court?"

I stood up, my legs shaking. "I want to thank the DPRK government," I said. "Thank you for giving me the letters and for allowing me to call my family. Thank you for treating me nicely."

I paused for a moment, then went on. "As you know, I have a four-year-old daughter. She needs me." At the thought of Hana, I started crying, the tears flowing down my face. "I need to be there for her," I said, my voice growing louder.

"Please have pity on her! She needs her mom! Please have compassion and forgive me!"

By now, I was crying so hard I wasn't sure if they could even understand what I was saying. "Please have pity on me!" I said. "Please, for my daughter's sake!"

I stood there crying, with my head bowed, not knowing what else to say. The judges left the room, saying there would be a short break. I sat in my chair, my head down, the tears continuing to flow. And then Laura came into the courtroom and sat down next to me.

We didn't look at each other for fear of being reprimanded, but I was glad to have her there with me. When the judges filed back in, they told us to walk to the center of the courtroom for the reading of the verdict, and we did as we were told. I held my breath. This was the moment I had been dreading for all these weeks.

I heard the judge say, "We hereby sentence you to fourteen years," and everything went black. I didn't faint, but I stood there in shock, unable to breathe. *Fourteen years? I can't survive fourteen years in prison!* I put my face in my hands and began crying loudly, for the first time not caring who heard me.

Laura said, "Oh my God, Euna," and hugged me, but the soldiers quickly separated us and led me out of the courtroom. I was crying and shaking, trying to take in what was happening to me. It wasn't the death penalty, but I would spend all of Hana's childhood in a North Korean prison. All because of the stupid mistake of walking too far across the icy Tumen River that morning in March.

When we got back to the guesthouse, Officer Lee came in to talk. "What did the judge tell you?" he asked.

"They gave me fourteen years in prison!" I wailed.

"Really?" he said, a look of confusion crossing his face. "No, it's twelve years. It was supposed to be fifteen, but you cooperated, so they reduced it by three years."

"No, I swear it's fourteen!" I said, but it turned out Officer Lee was right: It was two years for illegal entry and ten years for the "hostile acts" of working on a documentary about North Korean defectors.

And he had another revelation for me—a piece of information that I had missed when the judged announced my sentence.

The judge had said I would spend my sentence in "edification by labor." But I'd never heard this phrase in Korean before, so I didn't know what it meant. And by the time the interpreter read the sentence in English, I was too dazed to hear what was being said. But Officer Lee told me what the phrase meant: Laura and I were being sent to a labor camp rather than a regular prison.

Twelve years in a labor camp—could I possibly survive that long? I remembered stories told by former prisoners in which they described hunger verging on starvation, harassment, abuse, and backbreaking physical labor. I didn't know if I could take it, either physically or emotionally. How could

I bear being separated from my Hana until she was sixteen? Would she even remember me as her mother when we saw each other again?

And then I remembered something else. In the story of Sleeping Beauty I had been reciting for Hana every day at 1 P.M., the King and Queen send their beloved daughter away to protect her from the wicked Maleficent's curse. According to the curse, the daughter will be pricked on the finger by a spindle at age fifteen, causing her to sleep for a hundred years. So, to keep her safe, her parents decide to send her away until she turns sixteen.

I couldn't believe it—all these days, I had been reciting a story for Hana where the mom and daughter are separated until the daughter turns sixteen! And now that's exactly what was happening to us! A chill went down my back—I couldn't believe I had so blithely recited that story over and over. I felt like I had somehow brought our own fairy-tale curse upon us. What had I done? What would become of me now?

Eight

A NEW KIND OF WAITING

O N THE MORNING OF JUNE 9, I woke up sick. The stress of the trial, the weekend of waiting, and getting the verdict had all taken their toll, and I lay in my bed most of the day. Yet somehow, when I wrote to Michael that morning, I managed to convey a sense of optimism.

> *Iain wrote me a letter and he said think of every day as one day closer to you and Hana . . . I miss you so much . . . I miss Hana . . . I love you two. It's really sad that we have been apart so long, but the good thing is, we have hope and we know that we will be together some day. I love you. I wish you could hear my heart.*

Although I had been sentenced to twelve years in a labor camp, I felt surprisingly calm. I remembered the words of Ambassador Foyer when he said the trial might serve to open the door for conversation between the two countries, and I believed it might still be possible to go home through either amnesty or a diplomatic solution. After all, the DPRK government had needed to bring us to trial in order to save face, and they'd successfully done that. There's an old saying in Korea: Even a nobleman who hasn't eaten in three days will still use a toothpick while walking down the street. Saving face was tremendously important in Korean culture, and with any luck, the North Koreans might feel that in convicting Laura and me, they had succeeded in doing that and could let us go. At least, that's what I tried to convince myself, despite my deep distress at the verdict.

I decided to focus on God and trust that He would bring me home safely. My goal was to ask Him to bring me home before Hana's preschool graduation on June 26—a little more than two weeks away. I truly believed I would make it home by then, and I refused to let a sliver of doubt in.

I dreamed often of Michael and Hana in the days after the trial, and after Officer Lee brought me another package from Michael, I thought it might be a sign that the North Koreans would have mercy on Laura and me. At this point, I wanted to see everything as a sign of our possible impending release. On June 13, I wrote to Michael:

Honey, I dreamt of you again. I was so happy. We were home together and I believe Hana was there too. We were so happy. I am not sad . . . I believe my dream will come true very soon. I believe! I love you very much! I love Hana very much!

Around the same time, Officer Lee told me that Michael and Lisa Ling had made appearances on the *Today* show and *Larry King Live* on June 1 to make an open plea for mercy on us. At first, I was worried that their appearance on TV might have made the North Koreans angry, but when I asked Officer Lee about it, he didn't seem upset at all. I was relieved—and also glad that our families had taken that step after being silent for so long. Because there was no relationship between the United States and North Korea, I knew we needed people's voices rallying to our cause; otherwise, it was unlikely any progress would be made at all. And if enough people raised their collective voices, the U.S. government couldn't ignore them.

My friend Yasu sent me a letter with details of the *Today* show appearance:

Both the Ling and Saldate families went to NBC's Today Show this morning. The camera cut away to Hana a few times, and she seemed nervous and uneasy. Maybe traveling all the way to New York and to be on TV early in the morning made her a bit cranky.

Laura's sister, Lisa, did most of the talking, but Michael had the last word in the interview when the show's host asked him what Hana thinks of the whole situation. He replied, "Well, she still thinks her mom is at work." My heart, and I'm pretty sure the million viewers of the morning show's collective hearts, sank right there and then.

I hated that Michael and Hana were having to endure all this. I felt especially guilty that Michael, who had worked so hard to get his acting career off the ground, was finally getting on national television—but for the wrong reason entirely. Laura's husband, Iain, sent me photos of a vigil held in Los Angeles for Laura and me, and when I saw my dear husband's face, so serious and sad, in the crowd of people who had gathered, I felt numb. It was inspiring that so many people had rallied for our cause, but it seemed impossible that all this was happening for me. It felt surreal.

The optimism I felt in the days immediately after the trial didn't last. As the days ticked by and no further movement was made to set us free, daily life was an agony of endless waiting. I had hoped we wouldn't actually be sent to a labor camp, but it was beginning to seem inevitable. This felt especially true after a conversation I had with Officer Lee on June 19, when he told me we were entering a "difficult time" politically. Because I had access to DPRK news programming, I knew about North Korea's nuclear test in late May. Therefore it didn't surprise me that tensions had risen between the United States and the DPRK. And I feared the implication was that Laura and I would not be going home anytime soon.

And if we were sent to a labor camp, I didn't know how I could survive it. I had done research on labor camps for the documentary, and they are unspeakably brutal. Inmates are forced to work long hours of physically demanding labor. They're given very little in the way of food and medical care, and the living conditions are horrible—prisoners sleep in crowded, filthy rooms and are often beaten or harassed by guards.

I had read accounts of the camps from former prisoners, and they were similar to this—a former soldier's description, as quoted in a 2002 Human Rights Watch report:

> People in the facility were beaten every day with sticks or with fists. In the evening, they had to make time for an "ideological struggle" for one or two hours. This was an official time for the inmates to fight with each other and the guards indirectly provoke violence. The prisoners had to endure physical punishments, such as having to squat and stand up 300 times.
>
> There were many different ways of beating. Those who attempted to escape were held in a separate place. They were often hung on the wall all day long. Sometimes their hands were tied behind their back and they were hung on the wall for three to seven days. They were handcuffed and guards would stomp on the handcuffs.
>
> They would also use finger-cuffs, which tie the two thumbs together. As a result, the prisoner's fingers would

swell. If it was a political prisoner, his hands would be broken right after he was sent to the prison of the National Security Office. They would then be interrogated. During this, they would not be able to move at all. I witnessed these types of atrocities quite often.

In the same Human Rights Watch report, another North Korean describes his experience in a political prison where the inmates were abused and denied adequate food:

People tried to catch rats using shoes as traps, and then would roast and eat them secretly. What we were feeling was something beyond description as simply hunger. Salt was our only side dish. We ate leaves and grass if they weren't harmful, putting them in soup . . .

It was a savage's life, even though people there still had the minds of human beings. I cannot tell vividly enough how it was to be beaten. When our family moved there, we were surrounded by one hundred people and beaten. The police led people to beat us—newcomers must be broken in spirit this way . . . Officials beat so harshly that many of those people became disabled, or their legs were paralyzed, or they died.

In these places, there are no human rights at all for women. What they call sexual harassment in South Korea is nothing. What was going on was beyond description. Everything is exposed, it was nothing to have sex openly . . .

It may be better when a man is married, but as for women, they can't protect themselves in that situation. Even though a man might know his wife is having sexual relations with an official, he can't protest or talk.

The idea of spending twelve years in a place like this was too terrible to contemplate, and from this point on, I began offering up a new prayer: "Lord, when I am moved from this building, let it be because I'm going home." Officer Lee had mentioned that Laura and I might be moved to another temporary living space before going to prison, and he had said we might even be allowed to stay together, since Laura wouldn't have an interpreter at the new place. But although it would be a great comfort to be with Laura, I didn't want to change my prayer. Yes, being with Laura in a new place would bring me instant peace. Yet if I could be patient enough, and pray enough, I might receive the longer-lasting peace of being home. It wasn't easy to choose patience, but I forced myself to do it.

The next day, June 20, I was taken to a nearby hospital for a physical to determine whether I was healthy enough to begin serving my sentence. I had tried to stay as healthy as possible, walking every day in my room and eating the food I was brought, but I knew I'd lost weight and was feeling the effects of stress. I also suffer from rheumatoid arthritis, which had flared up during my captivity. But I had no idea how low or high the threshold was for being judged healthy enough to go to a labor camp.

To my relief, but also my dismay, the doctor determined that my health was too poor for me to be sent anywhere. I wrote to Michael that day, and included even more details, in case the North Koreans were reading my letters. I wanted them to think I was completely incapable of hard labor—even more so than the doctor had said.

The doctor told the prosecutor that I am not healthy enough to do any labor or live with a group . . . I don't think I will be capable of doing any hard labor. I couldn't even squeeze out my clothes after washing them. I feel like I am getting weaker and weaker every day . . . I tried to keep myself healthy but just all the stresses brought my weight down to 44 kg [97 lbs.] from 51 kg [112 lbs.]. I was never under 47 kg [103 lbs.] and this makes me worried.

The doctor said my liver . . . is not very healthy. That explains why I was having yellowish eyes . . . I will try to eat more and will try to take care of myself. A judge will make the decision if he will send me to labor camp or not next week. I really hope he/she will consider the doctor's opinion.

For the moment, at least, it seemed I was safe from the horrors of labor camp. But I also wasn't going home. I was stuck in an endless limbo—one that would become more and more maddening as the days went by.

❉

On June 21, the day after the doctor examined me, Officer Lee told me I would be allowed to call home for the second time. Just as before, we rode in a Nissan sedan to the Yanggakdo International Hotel, and he took me up to the same third-floor conference room with the beige phone. He told me I had ten minutes to make my call.

I had prepared a page of notes to make sure I wouldn't forget anything, and I placed it on the table in front of me before dialing Michael's number. To my great relief, he answered! It was hard to focus on important details when all I wanted to do was tell him I loved him, but I managed to let him know about my health issues and a few things he needed to know for Hana. I asked him to send me a few items—deodorant, some books, dental floss. I especially couldn't wait to get that last item, as I had been forced to pull threads out of my blanket to use for flossing.

It was so wonderful to hear Michael's voice—and this time, because I was calling while Hana was awake, I would get to speak with her, too! When Michael called her to the phone, I thought I might burst from excitement. I had waited for this moment for so long!

When she took the phone, she was silent for a moment. "Hana?" I said, "It's Mommy! Are you there?" I knew this had to be confusing for her—she was only four, and she hadn't seen me in more than three months. But I still wasn't prepared for the conversation that followed.

Hana and I spoke in Korean, which takes different forms depending on how formally the speaker wishes to address the listener. On the phone, she spoke to me in formal Korean, as if I were an adult she had just met rather than her mother. I was shocked. She had never spoken with me that way before, even when I asked her to as part of a Korean lesson, and I wasn't sure how to respond. In addition, she was telling me about a movie she'd seen—one I hadn't heard of—and I was having trouble following what she was talking about.

We spoke for a few minutes, and it was almost as if I didn't recognize the little girl on the other end of the line. Yes, she was my sweet Hana, but her voice was different, more mature somehow, and she didn't talk to me in that baby voice she liked to use with me. I wanted to cry, as I knew this was a sign that I had been away too long, but I knew I had to keep myself together for her sake. I told her I loved her and said she should be good for her daddy.

By arrangement with Michael, and with the permission of Officer Lee, I planned to call back after our first call finished, to leave a message for Hana so she could listen to my voice whenever she wanted to. But I had to take a moment to compose myself before making the call. I didn't want her to hear the sadness in my voice.

I called back, and when the machine picked up, I left my message in the strongest, happiest voice I could. "Hana, it's Mommy," I said. "Mommy misses you so much and thinks of you every day. I am far away for work and there aren't any telephones around here where I'm working. That is why I can't call you often.

"I will try to finish work soon, so until then, eat well and be a good girl for Daddy. When you miss Mommy's voice, ask Daddy to replay this message. I love you so much. Oh, and thanks for saving cookies for Mommy." Michael had told me that whenever Hana had cookies, she would set some aside for me.

I told her I loved her and hung up the phone, and the tears began to flow again. It was so hard to hear my Hana sound so distant, and to know I couldn't touch her and comfort her. In some ways, I felt worse after the call than before it.

Michael, too, was troubled by the call. The next day, he wrote me a letter that I would receive in early July. In it, he described his fears—and Hana's.

> It was very difficult to hear you so fearful. I cannot imagine what it must be like there. I only know that I feel only half alive here because you are there . . . I was really disturbed to hear that you lost 15 lbs. I told the State Department about your weight loss . . . [and] how worried I was, because you didn't have 15 lbs. to lose.
>
> Honey, I know I have asked you to be strong and I know that you have been . . . I can only imagine how hard it must be to stay strong, but you are doing a good job. I just want to let you know that the State Department is making progress in their talks with the DPRK.
>
> Hana cried this morning after last night hearing your voice.

She said she wanted to see mommy. I told her "soon," and that her grandmother and auntie are coming to stay with us. She was happy to at least hear that. But she wants to see you.

I wanted to see Hana, too, more than anything. I cried out to God, "You are my Father, and You know what Your child wants most at this moment. I would do anything for my Hana, and I know You want the best for me. Please send me home." But I just had no idea whether it would be days, months, or even years before that happened.

❖

In the weeks following the trial, I found some comfort in the fact that there were no more interrogations to endure and the crew who were looking after me—the two female guards and Officer Lee—now seemed more relaxed in my presence.

Since my earliest weeks in Pyongyang, Officer Lee had taken me for walks outside. This only happened two or three times a week, for about thirty minutes at a time, and the walks weren't scenic—they took place on a small, fenced-in patch of cement along the side of the building, about twenty yards long. But it was a luxury to see the sun and feel its warmth on my face, and once, after a late-spring rain, the breeze brought a wonderful grassy, earthy smell that reminded me of my childhood days, when my sisters and I would play outdoors at my grandma's house. For me, it was the smell of South Korea.

Such moments were disorienting. I was in captivity, yet my senses told me I was at home. Nevertheless, I drew comfort from these walks. They were the only time I really felt human during those weeks of detention, the only time I felt like a person rather than a prisoner.

I'm sure Officer Lee was under orders to take me for these walks, because he often seemed tired and inclined to skip them. He would sometimes ask me whether I wanted to go, and of course I always said yes. Occasionally, he even joked about it, saying, "I'm so tired, but whenever I ask, you never say no!"

Yet I suspect that Officer Lee liked these walks, too. Partly because he would let his guard down and talk about all kinds of subjects, especially after the trial was over. He was surprisingly knowledgeable about Western culture, and he seemed to enjoy talking about books, movies, and politics. He especially seemed to know a lot about American literature, frequently quoting the likes of Mark Twain and Margaret Mitchell in his criticisms of the United States. And he even told me something I didn't know—that "Mark Twain" was a pen name. I liked hearing Officer Lee's opinions about things.

He also seemed more amenable to answering questions about my situation when we were outside. I would ask him how things were going between our two countries and whether my situation was being affected by any geopolitical issues. I also asked him many times if I could see Laura, though the answer was always no.

One day, during a long conversation, he asked me if he was a scary figure to me during the interrogation. "Yes," I said. "When you were yelling at me, you were really scary."

"You know I was doing my job," he replied. "Are you scared of me now?"

I told him no, then asked, "Did you hate me?"

He said he did when he first interrogated me, but that after he got to know me and I admitted my fault and mistakes, he didn't hate me. At that moment, not for the first time, it seemed he almost felt bad that I was still being detained.

Once, I even felt bold enough to ask him, "Would you get into trouble if I told anyone you were nice to me?"

"No," he answered. "Why would I?" But I wasn't so sure.

Like Officer Lee, the guards slowly began opening up to having short conversations with me, and I began asking them questions. The older guard had been teaching the younger guard English, and I was surprised at how good her pronunciation was. I asked her what she wanted to do with her skills, and she told me she wanted to be an interpreter. "A lot of people don't know about our country," she said. "I want to learn English so I can work as an interpreter and present our country the right way."

The younger guard, who was very cute and often smiling, sang all the time. I had first noticed how beautiful her voice was not long after I arrived in Pyongyang, when I heard her singing "My Heart Will Go On," and I loved hearing her sing.

"Do you want to be a professional singer?" I asked her. "You could! You're really good!"

"No," she said, blushing. "My mom thinks I'm too crazy when I sing. Besides, I can just do it at work!" And she did, spontaneously breaking into song whenever the mood struck her. Culturally, this seemed to be a regular occurrence in North Korea—people often sang in front of their coworkers during breaks or lunchtime. Once, during a walk outside with Officer Lee, I heard a man and a woman singing in harmony nearby, in front of a small crowd. When they finished, the people clapped.

In mid-June, the younger guard got sick. She was weak and dizzy, and she could hardly walk. I felt terrible for her— all the more so because she was being forced to live here and watch over me twenty-four hours a day, seven days a week. I wished she could go home and recover, but the older guard seemed rather cold about her plight. "Just lie down and rest," the older guard told the younger one, who did as she was told.

The younger guard was lying on the couch in the guards' area, a place I wasn't allowed to be unless I was invited in. When the older guard left to report on the situation, I walked into the room and asked the younger one, "Do you need anything? Is there anything I can do for you?" She was uncomfortable with the fact that I was breaking the rules to offer my help, so she just shook her head.

The young guard may have wanted comforting, but for

obvious reasons it couldn't come from me, the convicted criminal. She was in such discomfort that tears began rolling from her eyes, and I began crying, too. I felt such compassion for her, and such frustration that I couldn't do anything. Once again, I was struck by how we were all ordinary people caught up in political rules. I wanted to perform the simple act of comforting this crying girl, but because of circumstances far beyond our control, I could not.

I had grown to care about this young girl, but even that small comfort was soon to come to an end. On one of our walks, Officer Lee told me that there was going to be a crew change, meaning that he and the guards would be replaced. I was really upset hearing this—not only sad that I wouldn't see him and the guards anymore, but also scared that the new crew wouldn't be as nice.

"Can't you stay with me until I get moved to the labor camp?" I asked him. As long as Officer Lee was here, I believed our status wouldn't change—but once he was gone, I felt, all bets were off. And I feared that if Laura and I were sent anywhere other than this guesthouse, we would have no more contact with the outside world. The Swedish ambassador wouldn't be able to visit us anymore and might not even know how to contact us, a thought that terrified me. I needed to have a connection—to know that someone knew where I was. And at that moment, apart from Ambassador Foyer, the only person I had was Officer Lee.

"No," he said. "Your status has changed. You're a criminal

now." He could see that I was upset, so he added, "Just feel lucky you weren't sent to prison right away. Usually, that's what happens. But we didn't want to send you and Laura into shock." I didn't feel grateful at all. I felt bitter that one of the very few things that gave me comfort was about to be taken away.

On June 24, the moment I had been dreading arrived. The two guards were replaced and Officer Lee told me he wouldn't be coming by anymore. "I'll ask them to treat you well," he told me, "but it won't be the same as our crew. You are a criminal now."

When the new guards came in, I could tell right away they were different. They were strict and unsmiling, and they spoke harshly to me when they spoke at all. The new officer, called a "Guarantor," was nicer than the guards, but talking with him was nothing like talking with Officer Lee. It was only about business, nothing else. The two guards now took me outside for a half-hour walk every day, but I walked in silence while they watched me.

My daily routine didn't change much, yet everything felt different. One of the guards was a stickler for cleanliness, and she would come in and inspect my floor for stray hairs. She also ordered me to keep the bathroom spotless, even though I had already been doing that for weeks before she arrived.

Just two days after the new crew arrived, the youngest of the guards, probably not more than 18 years old, came out of the bathroom and said, "That plastic bucket in there—you see how dirty it is? You need to clean it!"

"I've tried," I told her. "But I don't have anything to clean it with. The washcloth isn't enough."

She left the room, then returned a few minutes later holding an old toothbrush. "Use this," she said. "Make it clean." She thrust the toothbrush into my hand, turned abruptly, and walked out. I stood there, feeling the tears of anger and humiliation well up. I wanted to scream and curse, but I knew I had to be calm. The only way I could survive was by building a good relationship with these guards, so that's what I pledged to do. I went into the bathroom and scrubbed the bucket in silence.

As difficult as things had been in the first three months of my captivity, I could not have conceived of the mental anguish that lay ahead. In retrospect, the combination of losing Officer Lee and the psychological turmoil of waiting endlessly to be sent to labor camp became almost too much to bear. I began writing more and more—first on the backs of letters I had received, and eventually in a blank journal Michael had sent me. When I look at those writings now, starting in late June and moving through July, it's obvious that as time wore on I was moving to the brink of a breakdown.

June 27 marked another milestone I had been dreading. At 8 A.M. on that day, it would be 4 P.M. on June 26 in Los Angeles. And that was when my precious Hana would be getting ready for her preschool graduation—the event I had hoped and prayed and truly believed that I would be able to attend with her.

I was bitterly disappointed that I was still in North Korea, and overwhelmed with guilt that I was missing my daughter's first graduation ceremony. We should have been there together, to celebrate as a family—but I had ruined it. The only thing I could think to do was to spend the entire morning thinking of Hana and trying to picture her at the ceremony. I wrote to Michael during that whole period, marking the time as if I were there.

At 8 A.M., I wrote:

In an hour Hana's graduation will start. You know how much I wanted to be there for her . . . I hope she won't be too sad for me not being there for her. Please, could you please tell her that Mommy really tried hard to make it? Honey, from now on for two hours I will think of you and Hana like I am there for you guys . . .

At 9 A.M., I wrote:

It's 5 P.M. over there. I am looking at Hana's graduation picture. She's so cute in her gown. Are you nervous? I don't think the graduation will start on time but I can imagine that I am there next to you holding your hand and I am very excited to see her on stage . . .

I tried to send good thoughts, but I couldn't keep my fears from coming out, too. At 10 A.M., I wrote:

How did Hana do? Was she nervous on the stage? I think she probably did very well. She's your daughter and she has no problem standing up in front of an audience . . .

I miss you and Hana so much. Your last letter was so positive and it gave me hope that I might go home soon, but the week passed quietly as usual. No one informs me what's going on and I am afraid [of what will happen] if I need to stay like this another month . . .

❈

As June drew to an end, I felt myself sliding into depression. In my letters to Michael, I tried to stay positive, but it was proving impossible.

On June 29, I wrote:

I had a really bad day yesterday. I was so depressed and my body was totally possessed by my depression. I felt I was abandoned and was being killed in isolation.

I didn't specify it in my letter, but I felt abandoned by God. In all the letters and journal entries I wrote, I never referred directly to God or my faith, because I was afraid the North Koreans would read them and I'd get in trouble. But there were many times when I made references that only I would understand. I had truly believed that God would get me home in time to see Hana's graduation, but He hadn't. Why hadn't He answered my prayers?

On June 30, I wrote:

I don't know why, but I've been angry (or frustrated) for a couple of days. I am not angry at people, but at something. The fact that I am not with you and Hana makes my days harder and harder every day.

Once again, I was mad at God. After the disappointment of missing Hana's graduation, I had started praying again, asking Him to send me home when the time was right for Him. But as much as I tried to trust in Him, I was angry that yet another month was ending and I still had no idea when I would be going home. I just couldn't believe that God was keeping me in North Korea for yet another month.

On July 1, I wrote:

It's July 1st. I hate it. How could it be July already? I was hoping and hoping to go home last month. I had such energy and faith and belief that I could have gone home in June. Nothing seemed different yesterday and I felt so sick, so sick and then I wanted to yell at the sky, "Liar!" . . .

I feel guilty. I feel like I should punish myself or make myself miserable. Just knowing that you are sad every day, just knowing that Hana's wondering where I am. I feel like I should not be at peace . . .

My face is all puffed up. I hate it. I didn't even cry this morning, but my eyes are all swollen. I look horrible. I am glad you are not looking at me right now.

I even began having paranoid thoughts, wondering whether I'd been left behind and didn't know it:

For two days I had a weird thought. I felt like Laura had been returned to her family on June 29th. I just can't help myself thinking about that. And that makes me miserable. I'm glad if she really did return to her family, but why only her? Why do I need to suffer here by myself? . . .

I pulled myself together for three hours today and my mind is all over the place again, which drives me crazy. Why can't I be more calm and patient?

I tried to keep my mind calm, but with so many hours in the day and nothing to think about but how much I missed Michael and Hana, I just couldn't. The interrogations had been horrible, but at least they had been something to fill the hours. I tried doing meditation for a couple of days, but it didn't work. I read the books Ambassador Foyer had given me—classics like *Tom Sawyer* and *A Farewell to Arms*—but it was difficult to focus. I prayed almost nonstop, asking God to be with me and guide me.

When July came and I was still in North Korea, I decided I wasn't doing enough to get myself home—I hadn't asked God enough or cried out enough. I decided it was time to shout out for help, to do something drastic.

I set myself a goal of walking for seven hours each day, just pacing back and forth in my room, praying all the while. I chose seven for the seven days of Jericho, a story described in one of Hana's favorite gospel songs that we always listened to in the car. As told in the Book of Joshua, God instructs the Israelites to walk around the walls of the city of Jericho for seven days straight. On the seventh day, the Israelites walk around the city's walls seven times, then raise their voices in a shout—and the walls come tumbling down.

The story of Jericho is a story of faith and obedience. On the surface, it wouldn't seem to make much sense to conquer a city by simply walking around it, rather than attacking. There didn't seem to be any way the Israelites could win this battle, but God had a plan and the Israelites trusted Him. And when they did as He said, the walls of Jericho fell—just as God had promised.

I felt like I was facing an impossible battle, too, so this story really spoke to me. Maybe if I could be obedient like the Israelites, the walls of my situation would crumble and I would finally be sent home. For this reason, I chose Jericho as my touchstone. I began walking seven hours each day, spread out over several periods. I would walk a little before breakfast, more after breakfast, and a lot after lunch. As long as I walked a total of seven hours, I was fulfilling the plan.

When I was able to really put my trust in God and allow Him to lift the burden from me, I was able to find peace. But too many days I tried to take things on myself. I had to constantly remind myself that no matter what was happening, God was with me.

Fortunately, many of my friends from home had sent letters with Bible verses, and I drew tremendous comfort from them. A single verse could stick in my head for days, giving me strength whenever I thought of it. And sometimes several people would send the same verse, almost as if God had guided them to do it. I never asked for a Bible while I was in North Korea, as I assumed doing so would create trouble for me. So these verses felt like a gift from above.

At first, people had seemed afraid to send verses, fearing that the North Korean government might not respond well to overt displays of Christian faith. But when Michael asked our church members for prayers, he also asked them to send me letters, and many of them included Bible verses. They tried not to make it too obvious, inserting verses here and there within the text of the letters. But every time I read one, my heart would lift.

One verse that many friends sent was Hebrews 13:5: "Never will I leave you; never will I forsake you." At my darkest moments, when I felt more alone than I ever had in my life, I tried to remember these words. I didn't know it, but Michael, too, found solace in the same verse during my time in captivity. Thousands of miles apart, in an impossible situation that seemed to have no end, we both found strength in the promise God makes in this verse.

Another verse often came to mind when I prayed. In Matthew 17:20, God says, "Because you have so little faith, I tell you the truth: If you have faith as small as a mustard seed, you can say to this mountain, 'Move from here to there,' and it will move. Nothing will be impossible for you." I desperately wanted that mountain to move, and I clung to God's promise that my faith could help move it. Many times I would pray to God, "My faith is bigger than a mustard seed. You said it would move the mountain, and I believe You can send me home."

And there was one other verse that I turned to every single day of my captivity. Matthew 7:7 says, "Ask and it will be given to you; seek and you will find; knock and the door will be opened to you." I cried out these words every day, forcing myself to trust in their message and be single-minded in my focus.

I didn't know it at first, but Michael's request to our church also set in motion an amazing cycle of support. Our church members told their families and friends about Laura and me, and they went to their own churches to ask for prayers, too. Soon, prayer requests were spreading, person by person and church by church. In this way, people rallied for us across the country—an incredible outpouring of support that had its beginnings in the simple power of prayer.

I believed that God's promises were true, and I knew He could open the door for me. Holding to the strength of these verses, I tried to keep my heart open and my hopes up. But the hardest thing was accepting that God has His own time-table. I had to remind myself that He wouldn't ask me to bear more than I was mentally or physically able to—yet as the month of July wore on, there were days when I feared I was reaching that limit.

❁

On July 3, I woke up feeling sick. But as I wrote to Michael, I suspected that my illness wasn't caused by any virus:

> I've been so lonely and missing you and Hana. I think my mind is desperately missing you and causes this sickness . . . I don't know how much longer I can stay strong. I don't know why my hopes seem so light and vague. Am I getting really sick? I miss you. I love you. There isn't anything I think about during my days except wanting to be with you and Hana.

I let the guard know I was sick, as she liked to keep control over my situation, and proceeded to sleep about ten hours that day. The next morning, I felt better. But physical ailments still kept cropping up: an uncomfortable puffiness in my face, diarrhea, then constipation, a rash that spread over my back and shoulders, and even a painful hemorrhoid.

The strangest symptom I had was an unexplained hot feeling in my heart. I was having a lot of chest pain, which the doctor, who was visiting me once a week, had told me was a result of stress. But sometimes, especially when I was praying or calling out to God, I would feel an intense heat spread over my heart, like someone was pouring hot water on it. It wasn't painful or uncomfortable, but it was very odd, like nothing I had ever felt before. I wasn't frightened by the feeling, but it did make me a little anxious, since I had no idea what might be causing it. Was it a sign from God? If so, what was He trying to say?

Every day was a struggle to keep anxiety at bay. There wasn't enough distraction to keep my mind from wandering all over the place, and in the span of an hour, I could veer from feeling hopeful to anxious to sad and back to hopeful again. Because I was awake for so many hours a day, these cycles repeated themselves over and over and over again.

I began looking for signs, convincing myself that random occurrences might have some greater meaning. In Korean culture, the appearance of a magpie means good news will come, so whenever I heard the distinctive cawing of a magpie outside my room, my heart would leap. Once, when a guard opened the curtains so I could see outside, I told myself that if a magpie came right then, it meant I would be going home. And a magpie did come—but it flew right into the window and fell to the ground.

There were occasionally bugs in my room, including cockroaches that skittered across the floor. But there was one insect in particular that the guards always took note of: the money bug. These are centipedes, but not the cute and fuzzy kind pictured in children's stories. Money bugs look like big spiders with too many legs, and they like to crawl along walls. In Korean superstition, money bugs bring money, so killing them is bad luck. The first guards seemed to believe this, and they left the bugs alone. But the second crew would kill the bugs whenever they saw them.

I didn't kill the bugs, but I did take note one day when one was crawling up the wall. Once again, I thought to myself, *God, show me a sign. If that money bug falls off the wall right now, it means I'm going home.* At that moment, the bug did fall and I was instantly filled with joy—I believed at that moment that I would make it home after all. The feeling wore off quickly, though, as it always did with such "signs." As soon as I saw one, I always wanted to see another.

I also ascribed significance to certain days, focusing my energy and prayers on them in hopes that one of them would be the turning point in my captivity. Hana's graduation day was one. And July 7—lucky 7-7—was another. Even though I was trying to submit to God's timetable, in my heart I chose that date as the one where I'd be set free. And I prayed and hoped and wished as hard as I could that my wish would come true. I even had a vivid dream in which I told Michael to come pick me up on that day—a Tuesday.

The prosecutor came by to see me several times after the trial, and when he happened to come on that day, I wondered whether he was bringing the good news I was so desperate to hear. But instead, he said, "The United States government is not working hard enough to bring you home. We are not making progress." He also told me about a news story that supposedly quoted someone in the U.S. military asking why anyone should care about two journalists being held in North Korea when so many soldiers were dying in Iraq.

The prosecutor's words devastated my hopes once again. They also made me angry—at the U.S. government, at the North Koreans, and at myself. I was so frustrated that I just wanted to smash things, and I poured my despair out in a letter to Michael that day:

> *Every letter, you tell me to be strong. How long do you want me to be strong here? 12 years? I am sorry . . . I am not mad at you . . . I was very upset at the U.S. government . . . the reality is that the U.S. government won't yield anything to the DPRK government for us, and the DPRK government won't give us a pardon unless the U.S. apologizes to them.*
>
> *So here is the simple fact! I will be put in prison for so long. I am very upset. I know I am nobody, but my pain and family's pain are not nothing . . . I don't believe this is happening to me and my family. I really don't believe this . . .*

That afternoon, I got sick to my stomach, and I spent the rest of the day unsuccessfully trying to get ahold of myself as I slid further into despair.

I feel my head is spinning inside and I threw up . . . Poor honey . . . You still believe that I am coming home soon. Should I cheer you up? Yes? Oh, I am sorry. I threw up again. I will have to stop writing this . . .

I'm not crying. (I did earlier.) I am calm. I will be really calm, not pretending. I won't be mad at anyone, including the U.S. government and the soldiers who said, "Who cares about two Asian–American journalists in the DPRK when so many soldiers are killed in Iraq?" I see his point but tell him "Who cares? My family cares. Who cares? My daughter is waiting for me to come home. That's who cares, damn it!"

I am going to go [expletive] crazy here. Upset one minute and calm the next minute. Tell everyone [expletive] you! [Expletive] selfish people!

I was tormented by the thought of the suffering I was causing. I couldn't bear that my husband, my daughter, my family, should feel such pain. The burden was almost too heavy. I was beginning to buckle under the weight. The prosecutor must have seen I was close to a breakdown, because he sent the doctor in to examine me that night. Later they told me I could make another call to Michael—my third one—the next day. As soon as I knew I could talk to my husband and daughter, my soul became calmer. Just the sound of their sweet voices would give me hope and remind me why I needed to be strong.

When I called Michael on July 8, he sounded so happy to

hear my voice that my spirits soared. "Hana!" he said. "It's Mommy!" I could hear Hana start to cry in the background, and I said, "Put her on the phone!"

She took the phone, and through her tears she said, "I miss you, Mommy!" The words melted my heart, and I had to fight back tears of my own.

Michael had told me in a letter that Hana was really into Wonder Woman, so I said to her, "Why are you crying? You're like Wonder Woman, right?" She stopped crying instantly, surprised that I knew. "Wonder Woman doesn't cry," I went on. "She's strong! Like Hana!"

"Okay," Hana said.

"You have Mommy's voice mail, right?" I asked, meaning the message I'd left for her to listen to.

"Yes," she said.

"Whenever you miss me, just listen to it, okay?" I told her.

"Okay," she said. "I love you, Mommy."

I had never heard such wonderful words in my life, and I drank them in like a drowning woman. The ten minutes we spent on the phone that day brought me back from the brink—for a while, at least. Yet the waiting and wondering weren't over yet.

❀

As July wore on, I wrote more and more to Michael, pouring out my thoughts and fears in an endless stream. I tried to imagine being home with him and Hana, and I described happy scenes that I hoped would come true:

> *Just thinking about reading a book next to you in our living room makes me smile. I sit on the couch, and Hana leans on my side, sitting next to me. You bring us strawberry and banana juice and sit next to us with a book. A nice jazz LP is spinning on the record player and we get sunbeams through our sunroom windows. We are all happy and relaxed. And later, Hana and I fall asleep next to you . . .*

I also began letting my mind wander to foods I wished I could eat:

> *I want potato chips, Cheez Its, pita chips, pizza with lots of mozzarella cheese, bagel with cream cheese and tomato. I want a scoop of peanut butter. Oh, and milk, lots of milk, Coffee Bean's vanilla latte . . .*

I drew pictures of all of us at home, happy—of Michael surfing the Internet on his laptop, of us sitting on the couch together watching a movie, of me reading a bedtime story to Hana. I tried as hard as I could to focus on positive thoughts, as the alternative was just too painful. But no matter how hard I tried, despair would always creep in again.

The psychological effect of being kept in captivity, with almost no interaction with others, was profound. And what made it even worse was the open-endedness of it. When some-one is in prison, they know exactly how long they must serve before being released. But the situation Laura and I faced in North Korea was different. We knew we had been sentenced to twelve years, but we had no idea when—or if—that sen-tence would actually start and we'd be shipped off to a labor camp. Every day that we were kept waiting was a day when our imaginations were free to run wild.

On July 15, one of the guards pulled back the big, heavy curtains and opened the patio door to air out the room. At first, I was delighted—the sheer white inner curtains were dancing on the breeze as it came through the door, and I sat on my bed, watching with delight. It was a beautiful scene—and there was so much light flooding into the room! My spir-its lifted for a wonderful moment. But then I glimpsed myself in the mirror, seeing myself in natural light for the first time in nearly four months. I looked horrible—old, tired, with dirty hair and a hollow look in my eyes. The nice moment had turned bad, and all I could think of was that I was glad Michael couldn't see me like this.

Two days later, July 17, was the four-month anniversary of our capture at the Tumen River. On that day, the build-ing manager, happened to bring me some pretty yellow flow-ers she had picked. I was incredibly grateful, and even told her I had nicknamed her "Sunshine." She liked it, and her warm smile lifted my spirits that morning. But later that day, I began crying again, writing to Michael that I couldn't stop my tears. Back and forth, back and forth went my moods, and I had no way of stopping the pendulum.

On July 18, the prosecutor told me I would be allowed to call home again—the fourth time. But this time, I wasn't excited at the idea. By now, I was starting to wonder what the point was. The day before, the prosecutor had tried to explain that the U.S. government wasn't doing enough to help get us home, and he implied that I had to do something to change that. But I couldn't figure out what I was supposed to say or how I could change anything. As I wrote to Michael that morning:

> I really don't know what to say anymore. I already conveyed to you that the U.S. government isn't working hard for us . . . Oh, help me. Is there anything that I can do to resolve this issue? Even if I say it over and over, it seems nothing has been changed. What do I need to do? What should I tell you? How can I make the situation solved? I am desperate.

When I called Michael that day, he didn't pick up the phone, so I ended up once again calling my younger sister, Jina, as hers was the only other phone number I could remember. I begged her to tell me what I could do, then asked her for her help. "We need Michelle Obama's help," I said. "Can you help raise the voices of other moms? Ask them to write letters to her—she is a mother, she should understand! Maybe she will feel some compassion and ask her husband to help resolve the situation." It was a long shot, but I was desperate to find any new avenue for making some progress.

Jina told me that the U.S. government had admitted our transgression and apologized for it, news that made me nervous. If it was true, what were the North Koreans waiting for? Wasn't that what they wanted—for the United States to apologize, to help North Korea save face? Why weren't they sending me home? If an apology by Secretary of State Hillary Clinton wasn't enough to convince them, what would be?

As tears spilled down my face, I told Jina, "I can't spend twelve years in prison! I can't be separated from Hana for that long!" I felt defeated, and making things worse, Jina was absolutely quiet on the other end of the line. She didn't say the words she had said so often in her letters and in the other phone call we'd had. She always told me, "I believe I will see you soon," and her optimism always made me feel better. But this one time, she didn't say it. All I could think was, *Jina knows something I don't—something bad—but she doesn't want to tell me.*

I'm not going home, I thought. *I'm really going to the labor camp.* To top it off, the prosecutor told me the same day that Laura and I would be sent to prison "very soon." For the first time in this ordeal, I felt the complete absence of any hope at all: It now seemed that there was really, truly nothing I could do.

I wanted to scream, or tear my hair out, or smash things. Everything that had been building in me for months—the stress, depression, guilt, and anger—was poisoning me from within. I had never known such a feeling before, and the next day it manifested itself in a way I had never thought possible.

During my weeks in Pyongyang, doctors had given me various kinds of medicine to take. Some were for pain or stomach upset, and some were vitamins and supplements, like fish oil tablets and vitamin B pills. I didn't like taking medicine, especially if I didn't recognize it, and often I would only pretend to take it, washing it down the sink later when no one was looking. But there was one type of medicine the doctors gave me that I secretly saved: sleeping pills.

Every time I complained that I hadn't been sleeping, a doctor would give me sleeping pills and I would pretend to take them, too. Then I would hide them among the clothes in my vanity drawer. By late July, I had a handful. And while I didn't hide them with the intention to do harm to myself—in fact, I wasn't really sure why I was keeping them—I think they helped me feel at least a little bit of control over my situation.

On July 20, I walked for six hours and I could not stop dark thoughts from overtaking me. I would walk, then feel my nerves overwhelm me, then have to sit down to stop my heart from pounding. I would keep sitting until I managed to calm down, but then I'd feel the anxiety swell up in my chest again and I would have to get up and start walking. I just couldn't bear the thought of being away from Michael and Hana and asking them to wait for me.

Finally, I couldn't take it anymore. I took the pills from their hiding place and held them in my hand as I paced around my room. I just wanted to forget everything, to finally be at peace. All I had to do was put these pills in my mouth and everything would fade away . . .

But just at the moment I was about to take the pills, I thought about Hana. A picture flashed into my mind of Michael crying and little Hana standing behind him, confused and alone. How could I do this to her? How could I be so selfish? It would be easy for me to take these pills, to finally free myself from this prison I was in. But what would happen to Hana and Michael then? I struggled with my thoughts and feelings for a few moments, then returned the pills to the drawer.

At 10:30 that night, when I was an exhausted, emotional wreck, the Guarantor brought me packages from home. Once again, just as I was on the brink, I received a lifeline. Looking back, it seems like God knew exactly how much burden I could bear and He always provided for me just in time.

As I wrote to Michael that night:

Thank God [the packages] came to me today. I was really a bad girl today. I thought about bad things. I was so depressed and didn't want to make you wait for me for 12 years. I thought, if I don't exist, you will be free from this hard time.

But that thought made me cry so much . . . And soon I realized how selfish I was, thinking in that bad way. How would I be forgiven by my family and my daughter? I think I am a bit stronger person than I thought. I pulled myself together very quickly.

And I am okay now. I know I will cry again tomorrow morning,
but I am okay now.

That moment marked a real turning point for me. From
then on, I decided that no matter what happened, I was going
to make it through this ordeal. If I was going to prison, so be
it. Perhaps it was finally time to prepare myself for that possibility, rather than let the dread and fear of it consume me.

I had struggled to make my peace with accepting whatever God had in store for me. Next I had to do the same for
Hana and Michael. I realized that God would take care of
them no matter what happened to me. Whether I lived or
died, they would always be in His hands. Part of me hated the
idea that Hana and Michael would be fine without me, but I
had to trust in God. And the amazing thing was, five thousand miles away Michael was having a similar epiphany. He
decided to just put me in God's hands, telling Him that he
would trust God completely to take care of me—even if it
meant not seeing me for twelve years. Michael and I resigned
ourselves to God's will at almost the same time, and I could
feel the relief wash over me as I let go.

Three days later, on July 23, the doctor visited again to
determine if I was fit enough to be sent to the labor camp. I
overheard a couple of conversations that made it sound like
the prosecutor was pressuring the doctor—he wanted me to
start my sentence, and it was up to her to make me healthy
enough to go. I felt bad for her, as a doctor's role is not to

push a patient too fast. But she was obviously under enormous pressure to do what the prosecutor wanted.

She checked my pulse first while I lay on the bed. "Are you sleeping okay?" she asked. "And digesting your food?" I told her I was, and she asked about the ongoing pain I was suffering in my finger joints due to rheumatoid arthritis. Her tone was so gentle, her eyes so caring, that I started to cry.

"Why are you crying?" she asked.

"Because you remind me of my mom," I said. "I'm sorry."

"Why are you sorry?" she asked.

"Because," I said, "I heard you're in a difficult position, between my health status and the prosecutor's demands." I wanted her to know how much I appreciated her kindness, and that I regretted the fact that she was in this position because of me. But she answered simply, "It's okay."

So I told her about every single ache, pain, and feeling of sickness I had. When I told her about the chest pains I was suffering, she looked concerned. Without knowing the cause, it wasn't safe for me to undertake the stressful physical activity of a labor camp—so in the end, she determined I still wasn't ready to be sent away.

The waiting game would continue. But at least now, since putting everything in God's hands, I felt better equipped to deal with it. The question was, would I be able to keep up this outlook, or would I sink again into despair?

❈

On the morning of July 26, I woke up having just had a long, detailed dream with Michael and Hana in it. The dream wasn't about anything particularly meaningful—in fact, it was a funny dream where I was in a singing competition but forgot the words to my song. I was upset, thinking I would lose the prize, but then Hana joined me to sing along. She and I sang together, finishing with a great crescendo and raising our arms in the air like opera singers. Then I gave her a hug and a kiss, and I felt joy flooding through me.

As soon as I woke up, I wrote to Michael about this dream. After describing the whole thing to him, I had a sudden epiphany:

> Honey, it just hit me. Honor, career, all those things that I chased after are really nothing. They can't even be compared with the value of what our daughter means to us. There might be hard times, there might be some embarrassing moments as we live, but if you, Hana and I stand firmly next to each other to support each other, I think we will be okay.
>
> Thank you for always being there for me and Hana. Thank you for asking me to be your wife. I am very happy to know that I am your wife until death separates us. I am very happy.
>
> Love, Euna

For months, I had been driving myself crazy with guilt. But from this point on, I felt able to accept that God would guide my family and me. I was finally able to let go, to accept whatever decision He would make, rather than pushing for my own desires to be met.

At the same time, I suddenly decided to walk the whole seven hours of Jericho straight through, rather than resting throughout the day. I had never walked that much without stopping, but I wanted to show God how determined I was.

The next day, July 28, I walked and walked, pushing on even though my muscles ached and my body was exhausted. Incredibly, I was able to do the whole seven hours without a break. I was so excited, I referred to it in a letter to Michael—even though I didn't say exactly what I'd done, just that I had fulfilled a big task:

> It was a big day for me today. This morning I set a task for myself . . . and I did it. I am so proud of myself. I'll tell you later what I did. I feel like I'm a kid who's waiting for a prize after completing a task. I'm very tired but happy at the same time.

I didn't stop feeling frustrated, or angry, or sometimes even crazy. I still had pains in my chest and cried often. But these moments of revelation really felt like turning points: Family and faith became that much more important to me. And even though I was still stuck in this little room, just exactly as I had been for all these months, my world got bigger that day.

I resolved to hold on to these feelings as much as I could,

focusing on the hope that I would be home soon rather than the fear that I'd be sent to prison. Even when July finally gave way to August, I fought to keep myself from getting depressed. For every new month that started while I was in captivity, I had drawn a calendar so I could mark off the days. But I decided not to draw one for August. No longer would I count the days and weeks, feeling nothing but despair as I ticked them off.

Instead, I began writing an elaborate anniversary card for Michael, as our tenth wedding anniversary would be on the following Friday, August 7. I wanted desperately to spend it with him, of course. But I knew that God would only set me free when He was ready to do so. And that even if I wasn't with Michael on our anniversary, we would at least be together in spirit.

Nine

HOME AT LAST

O N SUNDAY, AUGUST 3, I awoke early, at around 5:30
A.M. Within ten minutes of getting up, I was already
writing to Michael, the first of many pages I would write that
day. At some point, I had decided to write every detail about
all my days to Michael, in case I didn't make it home. I wanted
him to know from my journal what my life had been like in
North Korea.

I told him about stomach troubles I'd been having, and
I described the plot of the book I was reading, *Anne of Green
Gables*. Later that day, after lunch, I told him I was feeling
particularly weak, as if I might faint. Still later, I informed
him that all afternoon I had been repeating aloud the same

sentence over and over: "I want to go to where Michael and Hana are waiting for me."

Ever since the new crew had come in six weeks before, this was a pretty typical day. But then, a little after 6 P.M., something very unusual happened: Officer Lee came to visit.

I hadn't seen Officer Lee in six weeks, but I had never stopped asking to see him. No one in the new crew ever really talked to me unless they were telling me to do something. And not only did I miss the interactions with Officer Lee, but I also knew he would tell me the truth if I asked him questions.

Officer Lee wasn't a good liar. Whenever he didn't have a prepared answer, he would hesitate before answering—but he never ignored a question. For all these reasons, he was an important figure to me, the only person I could get any real information from. I also was happy that he'd come because it meant that my request had finally been granted—which possibly meant that other requests could soon be granted, too. In my experience, one good thing often led to another.

When I was informed that Officer Lee had come to see me, I had a reaction that may seem strange but felt very natural to me. I was wearing a pair of gray sweatpants that Michael had sent, and I didn't feel it was appropriate attire for seeing a visitor. So I changed into something more presentable and combed my hair, then walked into the guards' room.

"I'm so happy to see you!" I said. But Officer Lee showed no emotion at all.

"How have you been?" he asked, his voice flat.

"Okay," I said as my smile vanished. I don't know what I expected, but of course Officer Lee couldn't show any happiness at seeing me, assuming he felt that way at all.

"Are you eating well? Sleeping well?" he asked.

"Yes," I said.

He nodded. "How are they treating you?"

"People are nice here," I said. "But it's been hard, because no one talks to me."

"That's because you're a criminal now," he said. "You have to understand, your status has changed."

When I didn't respond, he went on. "I'm here because you asked for me. Why did you want to see me?"

"I have a request," I told him. "Can I call Michael and Hana before I go to prison?"

"Yes," he said.

"And can I see Laura before we're moved?" I asked. For the entire detainment, I had never stopped asking to see Laura, but my requests were always denied. But this time, Officer Lee's response surprised me.

"I'll discuss it," he said. "We'll see." He paused for a moment, then said, "I'm here to inform you that there has been good movement on your case within the DPRK government."

My heart jumped, but I tried not to smile. His demeanor was very solemn, and it seemed inappropriate to express happiness at such a moment. I fought to keep my expression neutral and said, "Good news?" as casually as I could. "What is it?"

"It's just good news," he said. "It's going very well."

"Does that mean things are moving forward?" I asked, still not daring to hope that I might be allowed to go home. "Or is there a chance it could move backward?"

"There's no chance it will move backward," he replied. "It's moving forward." But that was all the information I would get from him today. "I have to take care of some business," he said. "I'll be back later." He left, and I was alone with my thoughts.

What was the "good news"? I was afraid to let my hopes get too high, but after so many weeks of waiting this was the first positive thing I had heard, and I desperately wanted Officer Lee's words to mean I was going home. As I wrote to Michael:

I am so exhilarated. I need to calm down. If I can see you again soon, I will feel like a person who found an oasis in the desert . . . Are we really going to see each other soon? Is it real? Too good to be true . . . I can't even express . . .

I waited anxiously for Officer Lee to come back that day, but he never did. I hardly slept at all that night.

❀

The next day, Officer Lee returned. "Did you have a good night's sleep?" he asked, a hint of a smile on his face.

"Yes!" I said. I was so glad he'd come back—and even happier to see the look on his face.

"You can see Laura today," he said. "Your request has been granted."

Relief and excitement flooded through me—I was finally going to get to see Laura! "Really?" I managed to say. "Thank you so much! Thank you!"

And that wasn't all. "You may be seeing someone from the U.S.," Officer Lee said.

"What?" I blurted. "Who is it? Are they here?"

"No," he said. "Not here yet. But just be aware."

"Do you know who it is?" I asked, my mind racing. Was it Michael? Was it Al Gore or someone else who might be working to negotiate our release? Ever since we were captured, I had hoped that Vice President Gore would get involved in the case, and earlier I had even told Officer Lee that I believed he would.

"I don't know," he said. "But it's someone very important." Once again, there was a hint of a smile in Officer Lee's expression.

I was still trying not to get too excited, but I'm sure he could see how happy I was. "Thank you so much," I said. "Thank you, Officer Lee."

"Just stay here in the guard area," he said. And with that, he left.

I sat on the couch in the guards' room, and after a short while Officer Lee returned. With him were two other North Koreans . . . and Laura! When she saw me, her mouth fell open—she apparently had no idea that she was being brought to see me. "Euna!" she said, and we both immediately started crying. We hugged each other tightly for several minutes and I felt a tremendous relief wash over me. I had never been so happy to see anyone in my life.

The very first thing I did was check her forehead to see how her wound had healed. To my surprise and relief, it looked really good. "Your head has healed so well!" I told her. "You won't need plastic surgery after all."

In the midst of our excitement, one of the North Koreans—Laura's interrogator, as it turned out—told us to go into my room because we were still in detainment. We walked in and Laura looked around at my living space. "You were here, in this building, the whole time?" she asked, surprised.

"Yes," I told her. I had figured out that she was in the same building during the interrogation and confession process, when Officer Lee kept going in and out of the room. But there was another clue that she was in the building: Once, I had noticed another guard doing yoga movements—the same kind Laura had shown me in the prison cell at the border—and I suspected the guard might have learned them from watching her.

I told Laura that I had even tried to send her a signal that we were in the same building. One day I'd thought I heard Laura talking with her interpreter as they came back into the building after a walk outside. So from then on, every time I came back into the building after my walks, I would ask my guard a question in a loud voice, hoping Laura would hear me. "Did you ever hear me?" I asked her. But she said no.

She looked around my room. "It's cleaner than mine," she said. "But your bathroom smells!" We laughed, and I thought how wonderful it was to have her here, in this room where I had been so alone for so long. I had spent so many days and nights here feeling despair, but now, having Laura with me, the room felt transformed.

The North Koreans brought us a lunch of cold noodles, and Laura and I talked and talked about our experiences in detainment. Laura told me that not long ago she had been sick for three days, even getting intravenous fluids. Unlike me, she had taken all the medicine she was given, but fortunately she didn't seem to have suffered any ill effects from it.

We talked about Ambassador Foyer, about the letters that kept us going, about the rituals we developed to try to keep our hopes from sinking. Laura told me that after the new crew came in, she was allowed to go running for thirty minutes every day. "I wore long underwear as my jogging clothes," she said, and I couldn't stop laughing at the thought of her running around outside in her underwear.

We talked and laughed for a while, and then the conversation turned serious. "Laura," I said quietly, "there were times when I hated you." I told her about my feelings of frustration when Officer Lee pitted us against each other. "There were times when I felt like I had to beg for my life," I told her. Then I had felt like we were on opposite sides. But now I just wanted to put it all behind us.

"Sometimes I hated you, too," Laura told me. "But I prayed for you every day."

"I'm sorry, Laura," I said, "but there were some days when I didn't pray for you."

"Euna!" she exclaimed, but she was smiling. I think we both understood that whatever had happened during this extraordinary period was already in the past. We had both been through a horribly stressful experience, but neither of us had any ill feelings remaining. Whatever disappointment or anger I had felt before was gone now, and I wanted her to know that.

"I'm sorry I didn't hug you back when you hugged me in the courtroom," I told her. "I thought we were going to see each other again."

"I thought so, too," she said. In the courtroom that day, neither of us had any idea it would be nearly two months before we saw each other again. And, of course, we had no idea it would be under these circumstances, with some mysterious visitor coming to see us. We both wanted to believe that we were about to be set free, but we were afraid to say so out loud, afraid to jinx it. "Let's not open the champagne bottle yet," I said. But there was no denying how excited we felt.

Shortly after lunch, an officer came and told us to change clothes. "Someone from the U.S. is here to see you," he said. Laura and I did as we were told—I put on clothes the North Koreans had given me, and she wore her own—and the two of us were separated again for the trip to the Koryo Hotel. The meeting was scheduled for 3:30 P.M., and we were as nervous as we were curious.

When we arrived at the hotel, Laura and I were both taken into a waiting room. The Guarantor was with me, and Laura's translator, a friendly young woman, was with her. As we sat waiting, Officer Lee came into the room and asked me, "Do you want some coffee?" He knew I loved coffee, but I had almost never been allowed to have it—in fact, in recent weeks I had taken to sipping hot water and pretending it was coffee. But obviously everything had changed, because now I was allowed to have it.

Laura and I tried to guess whom we might be meeting. Jimmy Carter? Bill Richardson? Al Gore? We knew it had to be someone high up, as Officer Lee had said it was someone "very important," but there was no way of knowing who. Suddenly, I was worried I might not recognize whoever it was! Would I recognize Jimmy Carter? Did he look the same now as he did when he was younger? And how do you address a former president—do you just call him Mr. President? My mind raced with nervous excitement.

At one point, I asked if we could go to the bathroom and the translator took us down the hall. After using the toilet, I went to wash my hands and noticed a familiar bug on the wall—it was a money bug! They really were everywhere.

"Did you have those bugs in your room?" I asked Laura.

"Yes!" she said. "The first crew told me not to kill them because it was bad luck, but the second crew killed them."

We both cracked up laughing—this was the exact same thing my guards had done! It was funny how Laura and I had gone through the same experiences even though we were separated all those months. As we giggled, I thought how wonderful it was to be able to laugh over something so silly. But I felt a little bad for Laura's translator, who stood behind us, confused as to why we were so amused by a bug on the wall.

All told, we sat in that waiting room for almost an hour. And although we were excited to be meeting with someone and hoped for the best, we still didn't know for sure if we would be going home. We kept asking the Guarantor, who was in the room with us, "Is the visitor here yet?" And he kept saying, "Not yet." Then he would joke, "Are you ready to go to prison?"—a joke that only he seemed to find funny.

As the minutes ticked by, I got more and more anxious, and soon the room was quiet. All I could think was, *Please let this happen. Don't let anything block us from this meeting.* My big fear was that there would be some complication and there would be no meeting at all—we'd just be taken right back to the guesthouse, dashing our hopes of release.

At long last, a man walked into the waiting room and told us it was time to go. We walked out into the hallway to find a number of men in black suits and wearing clear earphones. The thought flashed into my head that Officer Lee was right—this must be a very important person we were meeting. "Follow us," someone said, and we started down the burgundy-carpeted hallway, past the Baroque mirrors hanging on the walls. Everywhere I looked, there were serious-looking men with earphones.

We came to a big double door, and just as we walked up, it swung open. And there, standing before us, was President Bill Clinton.

I couldn't believe my eyes. He was tall, and his white hair seemed almost to be glowing, making him look like an angel. He looked at us with deep kindness in his eyes, and right away he opened his arms. Laura and I went straight to him and hugged him, and for the first time since that day on the Tumen River, nearly five months before, I felt safe. I started to cry, because now I knew for sure that we were going home.

"Thank you! Thank you!" I said through tears. I couldn't find words to express how relieved and happy I was at that moment—it was as if all the weight of guilt I had felt for so many months just lifted away from me. I felt flooded with joy, elated that this terrible ordeal was finally, mercifully, almost over. I had felt alone for so long, and now, standing here with me, was President Bill Clinton telling me we were going to be okay.

Through tears of her own, Laura made a request that she and I had discussed back in my room. "Please offer our apologies to North Korea," she said.

"It's all done," he said in a quiet, reassuring voice. He then went on to imply that we would be going home the next day.

We hugged again, and I thought my heart might burst from happiness. "Thank you!" I said again and again. These simple words seemed inadequate to express the gratitude I felt, but I couldn't think of anything else to say.

President Clinton gestured to a man standing nearby and told us he was a doctor. "He's going to ask you if you're physically okay to fly," he said. At that moment, I would have claimed to be well even if I was at death's door. When the doctor asked Laura and me if we were well enough to fly out the next day, we instantly said yes. I had never been so ready for anything in my life.

The meeting was very short, probably less than ten minutes. President Clinton, his aides, and the Secret Service personnel left, and Laura and I were alone in the room. Officer Lee came in and asked, "Well? What did he say?"

"We asked him to apologize to the DPRK for us," I said, "but he told us everything is done. And he said he had another meeting to go to now, but that he would see us tomorrow morning."

"That's it?" Officer Lee asked, his eyebrows raised.

That wasn't all, of course, but I suddenly realized I didn't want to tell Officer Lee the rest—that President Clinton had implied he would take us home the next day. Officer Lee must have known all along that we would be meeting with Clinton and that he would take us home. But he had pretended not to know. The North Koreans always wanted to believe everything was under their control, but here was one thing I could control—so I did. It felt like my own little secret.

"That's it," I responded to Officer Lee's question. Disbelieving, he asked me again—twice more. Each time, I said, "No, he didn't tell us anything else." Officer Lee just shook his head. It sounds like a small thing, but keeping that information to myself made me feel stronger. It was my first step toward not feeling like a prisoner anymore.

The North Koreans took us back to the guesthouse, and to our relief Laura was allowed to come back to my room. We were both incredibly excited, but we had noticed that no one from the North Korean side had told us we were going home. President Clinton must have known for sure that we were—and yet, until we had 100 percent confirmation from both sides, neither of us could quite believe it. It would be too devastating a blow to have it turn out not to be true.

During the 10:30 P.M. newscast that night, Laura and I caught a glimpse of Bill Clinton's face on the TV in the guards' room. We ran out into the guards' area so we could see the TV better, leaning forward to catch every word. Our eyes were glued to the screen as the news showed clips of President Clinton meeting with Kim Jong-il. It was true! They had met, and Laura and I were really going home!

Just after the newscast ended, Officer Lee came back—he wanted to make sure we'd seen the coverage of Clinton's visit.

"Did you see it?" he asked me.

"Yes," I said. He smiled. "Thank you for being nice to me," I said to him. He nodded slightly, then said, "Get some sleep," and left the room.

That night, Laura and I crawled into my bed and the two

of us giggled and talked half the night, like a couple of school-girls at a slumber party. We talked about the foods we'd been craving, and I told her about eating some candy the guard had brought me the night before. "I had been wanting candy so badly!" I said, laughing at the thought of it. I felt a little bad for the guards, who must have gotten no sleep at all, but we were too excited to sleep. I just couldn't believe we were really going home! After all we had been through, it seemed like a dream.

Around 2:30 A.M., we finally drifted into sleep. But it didn't last long: At 4 A.M. or so, I woke up. I felt more calm and peaceful than I had in months, and I wanted to have some quiet time with God. I walked to a chair by the window and sat there, silently contemplating everything that had happened. Everything I'd gone through already felt so long ago. I silently thanked God for watching over me through it all.

"Are you okay?" Laura called from the bed.

"Yes," I replied. "I'm okay."

I sat there, thinking about everything I had experienced in this place. So much had happened—so many ups and downs and emotional moments—and I knew it would be a long time before I could really take everything in. The day before, I had written this to Michael as I tried to sort out what it all meant:

> *I feel like I am living a new life and born again. I shall not forget this journey and I shall not forget the moments when I am grate-ful for all the things He has done for me.*

I still do not know why I was put on this task and what purpose He is using me for, but I will understand His will some day . . . I am sure.

❖

At about 4:30 A.M., a guard came into the room, turned the lights on, and barked, "Wake up! Wake up!" I jumped up, too excited to speak, and Officer Lee followed her in. "Did you guys sleep?" he said. "Time to wash and get ready to go!" He handed me three bags and said, "Pack your stuff!"

"I need to pack the things in my room!" Laura said, instantly awake. I gave her two of the three bags, since she had received a lot of packages through Iain's family in England, where, unlike in the United States, packages could be sent directly to the DPRK. A guard took her out, and I rushed to pack the things that were important to me.

Officer Lee brought in a big box and said, "Your books are packed—they weigh about fifty kilos. Do you want them?"

"No," I said. "We'll leave them here." Both Laura and I wanted to leave the books for people in North Korea who wished to study English, and we hoped that was where they'd end up.

"We also have some other things of yours," he said. He meant boxes of food and medicine that Ambassador Foyer had delivered but that we never received. "If you leave them, we'll just throw them away."

"That's okay," I said. I hoped the food and medicine would be used, but I didn't want to take them. I quickly put the few things I wanted into the bag—letters, photos, my clothes, a few toiletries, and the copy of the collected works of Charlotte Brontë that Ambassador Foyer had given me, which I wanted to keep to remember his kindness. The bag wasn't very big, so pretty soon it was full. But Officer Lee could see that I hadn't packed the North Korean clothes he'd given me over the course of my detainment, and I worried that his feelings might be hurt.

"I can't fit these in the bag," I told him, gesturing to the winter coat, brown canvas pants, and shirts.

"What," he said, "you don't want to take them because they're not as nice as your things?" He seemed disappointed, and he gestured to a fabric bag that Ambassador Foyer had sent with items from home. "You can fit them in there." I packed the clothes in the fabric bag, even though I knew I would never wear them, or maybe even look at them, again.

"Wear something clean," he said. "Someone very high up in the DPRK government is coming to meet you." I had on jeans and a red shirt that Michael had sent, but no one really wore jeans in North Korea. I didn't want to change, but it was curious to me that Officer Lee still seemed to feel that even now my appearance might reflect on him.

After I'd finished packing, he said he wanted me to talk with him for a moment. He gestured to one of the chairs in front of the desk in the guards' room, and I sat down. "If you get sent home," he said, "who made that decision?" Despite his use of the word "if," I knew for sure after meeting President Clinton that we were going home, so I wasn't scared.

I knew what he wanted me to say, and so I said it. "Of course, the DPRK," I answered.

"Don't forget that," he said. "Without our generosity, this would never have happened." Just as I had during the interrogation, I felt compelled to respond as he wanted me to, whether it was true or not. I think Officer Lee knew I was just saying the words, and that I would say something different after I was home. But it was almost like tying up the last detail—the DPRK wanted us to thank them, and so we would. And then we would be free.

"Let's go," Officer Lee said, and I walked out of the guards' room for the last time. At that moment, it hardly seemed possible that I would never see it, or the bedroom where I had spent so many solitary, agonized hours, again.

Officer Lee and I proceeded down the hallway and outside the building, passing by the paved area where we had taken so many walks. Then we entered a gate into another part of the building, and he took me into a small room with a desk and a few chairs. Two members of Clinton's team were there— John Podesta and Doug Band—as was a camera crew. Laura and I were seated next to John and Doug.

Two generals in their fifties, wearing army uniforms and with their chests full of medals, walked into the room. Shortly afterward, Laura and I were asked to stand and one of the generals read a pardon note on behalf of Kim Jong-il. This was a serious moment, but as the general read the statement, I felt completely relaxed. I didn't listen closely to the formal Korean he was reciting, but just kept thinking, *This is it! This is really it!*

When the general finished the statement, cameras clicked to record the moment. And just like that, it was time to go.

As we walked out of the room, I saw Officer Lee standing there. He didn't say anything to me, but he was smiling. Laura and I were taken back to our rooms and Officer Lee came in. He asked me to write a thank-you letter to the DPRK government and its leader, Kim Jong-il. I did as he asked, and when I handed him the letter, he said, "That's it! You're going home."

I felt a flood of gratitude to this man who had treated me humanely despite the politics of our situation. The kindness I had seen in Officer Lee's eyes that very first day in Pyongyang had turned out to be real, and I knew I would never forget him.

I went to hug him, but he stepped back immediately. I was disappointed, but not surprised. Even though I had been pardoned, it would still have been a breach of custom for him to embrace me.

"It's not our way to say good-bye," he said, official to the last moment.

"Do you want me to bow, in the Korean way?" I asked him.

"No need to," he replied.

I looked at him with tears in my eyes. "Thank you," I said emotionally. "I thank you for your generosity."

"Be well," he said, smiling. "And don't ever do that again."
I laughed, and promised I wouldn't.

I walked to a waiting Volkswagen Jetta and put my bags in
the trunk, and then, just as I was about to get in the car, I saw
Sunshine, the building manager, standing with a colleague. I
rushed over to her and took her hand. "Thank you so much
for your kindness," I said, feeling true warmth for this woman
who had treated me better than anyone.

She smiled. "Good-bye," she said simply, and I turned
back to the car. No sooner had the exchange happened than I
thought, *Should I have done that? Will she get into trouble?* Even now,
at the very end of my experience in North Korea, I couldn't
help but worry about the consequences of my actions and the
complicated politics of it all.

I climbed into the back seat, where Laura was already sitting, and looked out the window to see Officer Lee and Laura's
officer waving to us. Laura waved back, and I bowed my head
Korean-style. The car pulled away, and that was the last I saw
of them. We were going home.

At the airport, we got out of the car to find a crowd of
photographers waiting for us. As flashbulbs popped left and
right, we waited for President Clinton to arrive and board the
airplane first. He walked up the stairs to the plane, and after
a few minutes Laura followed him up. I went next, climbing
the steps as if in a dream.

Laura was bubbly and elated, talking and smiling the
whole time, but I was very quiet. It was like coming out of a

dark place and into the bright sunshine, when your eyes need time to adjust. I was adjusting to the new reality of my life. But nothing would be real until I could touch my baby and Michael. Right now, I was just in a strange limbo, no longer trapped in detainment but not yet free.

It didn't seem real that this was actually happening after so many months of waiting, and as I boarded the plane it was as if a deep peace was settling over me. Once we got on the plane, though, and I was given the chance to call Michael before we took off, I got excited.

I dialed Michael's number, and he picked up right away. "Honey, I'm coming home!" I said. "I'm in the airplane! I can't wait to see you!" He already knew about President Clinton's trip and that I would be coming home.

"I can't wait to see you, too!" he said, then added, "Have you left Pyongyang? Are you in the air?"

"Not yet," I said. "We're still here."

Michael was apparently as eager not to jinx things as I was, because the next thing he said was, "Okay, call me when you're in the air! I want to know you've *really* left and are really coming home!" I laughed and promised I would.

❀

The first leg of our journey home took us to Japan, and Laura and I sat next to President Clinton for the short flight. He told us that his daughter Chelsea had urged him to make this trip, pointing out that he would have gone if it had been his own daughter there. "She's not that much different in age than you two are," he said.

President Clinton was thrilled to take the lead in getting us released. He told us, "I feel blessed to have been able to help. It feels so good to be able to bring you two home." We just kept thanking him, unable to believe our good fortune. It was so surreal to go from being alone in the guesthouse room for days on end to sitting next to President Clinton on a private jet, flying home at last.

We stopped at a U.S. military base in Japan to refuel and had breakfast there. Eggs, fresh fruit, waffles, coffee—and not a grain of rice in sight! A member of President Clinton's team, David Straub, told us not to eat too much, as the sudden change in diet would give us digestive trouble. I tried to heed his suggestion, but it was exciting to finally have Western food!

On the long flight from Japan to Los Angeles, we needed to prepare for the very public homecoming that awaited us. There would be camera crews at Bob Hope Airport in Burbank, so we'd need to make a statement of some kind. At first, we were both going to speak, but after Laura drafted her statement I saw that it spoke for both of us. It would have seemed repetitive for us both to say the same thing, so we decided Laura would give the only statement.

This was okay with me for another reason, too—the truth is, I've never been very comfortable in front of cameras. In fact, I was eager not to be recognized after we returned, and I even thought about wearing my reading glasses as I got off the plane, as they would help hide my emotion and make me look a little different. I just wanted my life to go right back to normal—right back to what it was before this whole ordeal began five months earlier. But that was impossible, of course.

I wrote my last note to Michael just a few hours before we arrived in Burbank. The final lines read:

> *Laura made a nice statement and will speak for both of us and I thanked her for working on it for us. I told Laura that my problem always was meeting new people, and she told me not to lock myself in. After all these experiences, I shouldn't worry about anything, and I hope God will be with me for my new step to my new life.*

At long last, we could see the coast of California—home! The sun was rising, casting an orange glow over Los Angeles. It was a beautiful, incredible sight. As we began our descent into Burbank, President Clinton beckoned us to come look out the cockpit window. "I just want to show you something," he said. We peered out and could see a crowd of people gathered on the tarmac, many with cameras. "That's how many media there are," he told us. "So you won't be surprised."

Suddenly, I caught sight of Michael and Hana. "That's my baby!" I exclaimed, elated to finally be seeing her for the first time in so many months.

"Can you see her?" President Clinton asked, excitement in his voice. I felt the tears spring to my eyes as I said, "Yes!"

We had agreed that Laura would deplane before me, but now she asked me with a smile, "Are you sure you want me to go first?"

"No!" I said. "Can I go first?" I just couldn't believe that in a few moments I would finally be holding Michael and Hana in my arms—the moment I had dreamed of for so long. As the plane landed and we all waited anxiously for it to taxi to a stop, the mood on the plane was one of elated anticipation. This was it! We were here! And now we'd get to have the best moment of all. Finally, the plane rolled to a halt and the door opened.

When I looked out and saw all the people gathered— all the family, friends, colleagues and other people who had supported us—I was filled to overflowing with gratitude. I walked just a few steps down the airplane's stairs, then stopped and bowed deeply in thanks. From a very young age, I had learned to bow to express gratitude, and it came out naturally.

There's no way to express the utter joy I felt when I saw the two loves of my life waiting for me at the bottom. I hurried down the remaining steps, and when I got to the tarmac Michael enveloped me in a big, warm hug as I knelt down to embrace Hana. For a moment, she hesitated, overwhelmed. It was painful, but I understood—five months was a very long time in the life of a four-year-old, and all of this had to be confusing.

I didn't want to force her to come to me—I would wait until she was ready. I just opened my arms and said, "It's Mommy. I'm here. Do you remember Mommy?" As I looked into her precious face and saw the uncertain look in her eyes, my heart melted.

Hana nodded her head shyly.

"I missed you," I said, holding her little hands in mine. "Can I give you a hug?"

She reached her arms toward me, and I gave her the biggest, most deeply felt hug of my life. Michael bent down and embraced us both, and I sobbed. I had never felt more love, and I wanted the moment never to end.

More hugs followed—from Laura's sister Lisa, her husband Iain, Al Gore, Michael's dad Frank and his stepmother Karen, and many other people. And through it all I carried Hana, who now clung to me in a tight hug, as if she feared I might disappear if she let go. Eventually, President Clinton came down the steps of the plane and joined us on the tarmac. He and Al Gore embraced, and we all just kept hugging each other until Laura walked to the podium and gave her very eloquent statement, thanking everyone and asking for our privacy in the days ahead.

After Laura's speech, I overheard President Clinton saying to Al Gore and the CEO of Current, Joel Hyatt, "You need to give these girls a raise!"

Joel just smiled, but he got his own joke in a little while

later, after things had calmed down and the crowd had started to dissipate. He leaned toward me and said, "So how did you like your first assignment?"

"Unforgettable," I said, and we all laughed. The best thing about this assignment was that it was over. Finally.

EPILOGUE

Aᴏᴛᴇʀ ᴏᴜʀ ʀᴇᴜɴɪᴏɴ at the Burbank airport, Michael, Hana, and I got into the back seat of my red Pontiac Aztek for the ride home. Michael's father, Frank, was driving and his stepmother, Karen, was in the front passenger seat. They had come from Fresno to support Michael and help him get our apartment ready for my arrival.

As we rode along the streets of Los Angeles, everything came back to me quickly; the signs advertising gas prices hadn't changed much, and cars zipped along the streets just as they had when I left on that sunny California day back in March. All I could think was, *Was I really away from all this for almost five months?* It didn't seem possible that I had been away for so long—and it was especially surreal to think that I had been in North Korea.

Hana was sitting next to me in her car seat, holding my

right hand, and Michael was on the other side, holding my left. We all clutched our hands tightly together. I had pretended to hold their hands so many times while I prayed in North Korea—but this time it was finally real! Hana's little hand was so comforting and soft. I kept rubbing her fingers, and she did the same to me. And Michael held my hand tight, not letting go until we got out of the car.

When we arrived home, a simple banner hung in front of our apartment building with the words "Welcome home, Euna." It was such a wonderful feeling to be welcomed and accepted, and the line "There's no place like home" popped into my head—a line I had quoted many times after watching *The Wizard of Oz* with Hana. But the banner, which our friends Paul and Kristine had put up, wasn't the only thing waiting for me. When we parked in front of our house, I saw a crowd of media people. This wasn't the scene I expected, but I didn't feel too nervous, thanks in part to something President Clinton had told me.

During the flight home, President Clinton had shown Laura and me news articles about us. I knew many people had been rallying and having vigils for us, but it was still overwhelming to read about it all. "I'm nervous about being interviewed," I told him, "but I don't want to be rude to the people who helped keep our story alive." I knew that without press attention to our situation, we might not have been released, and I didn't want to seem ungrateful. President Clinton nodded, then gave me a piece of very wise advice.

"You shouldn't feel obligated to do interviews," he told me. "You can just say, 'Thank you for your interest, but I'm not ready to do an interview right now.'"

When I got out of the car, I told a female reporter who approached that I was sorry but I wasn't ready to talk just yet. I headed quickly through the door into our apartment building, and Michael waved to the reporters and said, "We're glad she's home, and thank you, everyone, for your support."

When we reached our apartment door, my father-in-law asked me if I wanted to unlock it. I immediately said yes. For so long, this was something I could only dream about doing! I unlocked the door and opened it just as I had nearly five months earlier, before this whole ordeal happened. I was finally home.

As I looked around our apartment, it felt like I was seeing in snapshots. The rooms were just as I remembered them, and the furniture was in the same place as when I had left. Yet, although nothing had really changed, everything felt different. Water stains on the sand-colored sofa and ottoman caught my eye right away, and I felt a stab of guilt. It was as if these stains told me the story of how Michael and Hana's days had been, and of how Michael had struggled to hold their lives together while I was gone.

Like a filmstrip, I could suddenly see how Michael's days unfolded: He would sit at the computer, searching for any news about me and then sending e-mails to people asking them to write me letters. He'd communicate with Laura's family and the State Department, hoping for any sign of progress. Then, after all that, when he picked up Hana from school he would try to keep her happy—to keep her from knowing how frightening and difficult this time was for her parents. Then he might sit on the couch to watch a movie or play video games, because he couldn't sleep and needed to keep his mind occupied. It must have been such an ordeal for him, and at that moment, looking around the apartment, my heart went out to my husband.

Frank and Karen had helped Michael clean the apartment, but there had obviously been more than they could do in such a short time. They left soon after driving us home, so we could rest, and Michael told me he wanted to take a nap. "I finally feel like I can sleep," he said. Hana needed a nap, too, since she'd gotten up so early in the morning to come greet me at the airport. I could see the exhaustion in their eyes, and I was so happy they could finally relax.

But I wasn't ready to rest yet—not as long as those water stains were on the couch. They may have just been ordinary water stains, but to me they felt like much more. They represented the difficult time we had been through. And I wanted to clean them up, to make them go away without a trace.

While Michael and Hana slept, I cleaned the whole apartment. I swept and dusted every corner, cleaning everywhere I could reach. As I wiped those stains from the couch, it was as if I was trying to wipe away any stain that was left in my family and me. This was my way of trying to get back to a normal life as soon as possible—we had missed nearly five months, but I wanted everything to be just as it used to be. I cleaned and cleaned that day until my body gave up in exhaustion.

While I was cleaning, I checked on both Michael and Hana. As I stood next to Hana's bed, looking down at her, a tremendous feeling of grace came over me. Then she opened her eyes slowly and looked up at me. I smiled. But suddenly she got a sad look on her face and turned her back to me. It was as if she thought she was seeing me in a dream and it made her sad.

I burst into tears and bent down to take Hana into my arms. I held her tight, saying, "Hana, Mommy's here. Mommy's here." She didn't move, but just fell right back to sleep in my arms. No matter how badly I wanted everything to be normal again, it obviously wasn't going to happen right away.

My sisters Mina and Jina had wanted to come to Los Angeles for my arrival, but they decided to wait out of respect for the space Michael, Hana, and I needed. But I called them that day to thank them for their unconditional love and support and for being wonderful sisters. We made a plan to all get together in L.A. within two weeks. Next, I called my parents in Korea. They were both calm, and our conversation felt as normal as if I'd never been detained. I apologized to each of them for any pain I had caused, and I thanked them for their prayers. It was such a joy to talk to my loved ones without having to carefully choose my words.

Two days later, on Friday, August 7, Michael and I celebrated our tenth wedding anniversary—a big occasion for any couple, but for us an event that meant so much more. Michael wanted to go out and do something special, but I was so happy just to be with him and Hana that I didn't ask for anything else. The three of us had dinner together at Hana's favorite Korean restaurant, and I marveled again at how much joy I felt at simply being with the people I loved.

That Sunday—the first Sunday since I had been home— I went to church. It's hard to describe how wonderful it felt to be able to pray openly after so many months of doing so silently, or in secret. I felt so blessed the whole service, and I could feel God reminding me that He had answered my prayers. When we sang a gospel song called "You Came to My Rescue," the tears streamed down my cheeks:

> *My whole life*
> *I place in your hands*
> *God of Mercy*
> *Humbled I bow down*
> *In your presence at your throne*
>
> *I called, you answered*
> *And you came to my rescue and I*
> *Want to be where you are*

So many times in North Korea, I had cried out in anguish, sadness, or fear. But now I cried out to God how thankful I was. I knew He heard me and understood what I had been through. And because He understood, I was not ashamed to cry.

❈

I soon got back into a daily routine, taking Hana to her preschool, ballet class, and the bookstore. Throughout the endless months in North Korea, I had dreamed of these moments—moments that before my detainment I wouldn't have treasured nearly so much. I had always been the kind of mother who let distractions creep into my time with Hana, and the kind of wife who came home too exhausted from work to do anything but flop onto the couch. I had pushed so hard to achieve things in my career, believing that by doing so I was helping my family. In the process, I had forgotten what was truly important in life.

But since I've been home, I look at life very differently. Now, when Hana asks for me, even if I'm working, I'll close my laptop and give her my full attention. When Michael needs something, I look into his eyes as he speaks. No more half-listening or wandering thoughts—my family deserves so much more than that. They're the most important thing in the world to me, second only to my relationship with God, so why not treat them that way? And funnily enough, now that I have learned to give them my full attention when we're together, I don't feel guilty anymore when I *do* need to work.

I didn't suddenly become the perfect wife and mother,

though—far from it. I still struggle with impatient feelings and forget sometimes to slow down and enjoy the life I have. But then I think back to how I felt in that room in Pyongyang. I remember the desperate desire I felt to once again enjoy the simple joys of loving my family and knowing that they love me. As terrible as it was to endure all those months of separation, being apart from my family also gave me a gift: the gift of appreciation for what I have.

The days since my detainment have passed by quickly, but some things from that time have remained with me. I often think of the people who were there with us through our difficult time. I never met most of them, but in my heart they became my friends. I wanted to contact everyone who showed us support, but as I got busy trying to track them all down, I realized I was once again spending too much time away from my family. So one day I closed my computer and decided to wait to thank people. But there was one thing that I didn't want to wait to take action on.

On July 28, the day in Pyongyang that I walked the entire seven hours of Jericho without resting, I felt such gratitude toward God for giving me that strength that I made Him a promise: When I got back home, I would go to church and share my experiences with people there. God had stayed with me and kept me safe throughout my ordeal, and now He had delivered me home. So it was time to fulfill my promise to Him.

I called the pastor of my church, Pastor Tim, and told him my plan. I shared with him how the verse about the mustard seed had kept me going, and how I desperately held on to the verse "Ask, and He will answer." And I told him I wanted to share what I had learned from my time in North Korea with the congregation.

I had never done any kind of public speaking, so this was not an easy promise for me to fulfill. Though I knew in my heart I needed to do it, just the thought of standing and speaking in front of some 750 people made me nervous. Through conversations with Michael during my detainment, Pastor Tim knew I was an introverted person, so he told me to take my time—there was no rush to do the speech. But I knew I had to follow through on what I'd promised. So we agreed on the date of Sunday, August 30, nearly four weeks after I arrived home.

The closer we got to that Sunday, the more nervous I became. That morning, I stood on the stage in front of the church, with Michael on my right and Pastor Tim on my left. Silently, I offered up the same prayer I had said while standing in the courthouse in Pyongyang, asking God to speak through my tongue. In the DPRK, there had been no one to support me as I stood in front of the judges. But here at our church in Los Angeles, I felt an incredible amount of love and positive energy from the people sitting out in the congregation.

I gave my testimony that morning, and although there was a moment when I cried and the congregation cried with me, I still felt happy. I had fulfilled my promise to God, and I felt He was proud of me. It was a wonderful moment.

Yet there were painful days during this time, too. A few weeks after we returned from North Korea, some people began publicly blaming Laura and me for what had happened there. We were criticized for allowing ourselves to be in a situation that led to our arrest, and for the fact that some materials for our documentary ended up in the hands of North Korean and Chinese authorities. Some accused us of making things more difficult for the very people we had wanted to help—the activists and defectors whose stories we sought to tell.

These were difficult days. People asked: Should I have trusted our guide? Why did we even go to the river at all? Did we underestimate the risk? They wanted answers. I understand. During my incarceration and since I have been home, I have asked similar questions of myself. But I honestly don't know when—or even if—I will have satisfactory answers. My perceptions of the decisions I made leading up to, on, and in the aftermath of that fateful day have been irrevocably colored by the consequences that ensued.

What I do know for sure is this: At the time, the decisions I made—on my own and with my colleagues—felt right. As journalists, we went to the heart of a story we believed needed to be told. We were striving to bring to light circumstances few viewers would have context for understanding. In seeking to make our reporting as truthful and powerful as it needed to be, we made choices that, in retrospect, were perhaps unwise.

Because our work on the documentary didn't turn out

the way I expected, I became very sensitive to how well-intended actions can cause negative consequences. I wasn't able to complete the documentary, which would have told the story of the North Korean defectors and shed light on their lives. And in the process of trying to do something good, I might have made someone's situation more difficult.

Although some people criticized Laura and me, many others encouraged us to keep going. As one person noted, the activists and North Korean defectors were never going to be in an easy situation; we needed to salvage something good from what had happened, rather than hide from it. In my heart, I still wanted to help them. But I needed to wait until a door opened for me to tell their story. And then I got the opportunity to write this book.

Writing this book is my way of completing the documentary. It has given me the chance to not only finish telling the North Korean defectors' story, but also to share how God carried me throughout my time in the DPRK—whether I was focused on Him or not. Whether I was weak or strong, angry or calm, His presence was constant. I may not always have seen it at the time, but just as in the poem "Footprints in the Sand," it was during my most difficult moments, when I felt completely alone, that He was actually carrying me through. Otherwise, I'm not sure I would have made it.

I learned that God's love is consistent even when I'm not paying attention to Him. Even when I hurt Him, when I yelled at Him or doubted His reasons for decisions I disagreed with, He never left me alone. This story of the most difficult time in my life will always be a reminder of His enormous love for my family and me.

It's strange that it took those months of imprisonment, trapped within the same four walls, for my world to finally become bigger. My understanding of people has grown; instead of judging others, I now try to see things from their perspective. And the people who stepped out of their comfort zone to help us, despite all their own concerns, are now a part of my world. My understanding of God has grown, too. I have learned that I cannot rely on what the world promises and the financial security that work brings me, but only God can provide real, eternal joy.

I hope that, in some small way, sharing my story might help open up the world for others. And maybe, one day, I can share it with the very people who brought me here—the North Koreans whose stories I sought to tell.

Acknowledgments

This book started because someone believed in my story. To my agents, Jennifer Gates and Todd Shuster from Zachary Shuster Harmsworth: Without you, this book would not be here today. Thank you, Jen, for your nurturing and patience in dealing with all of my crazy questions, and Todd, for your wise advice. I am grateful for your unbelievable support.

My agents were the ones who started the book, but my husband, Michael, was the one who dealt with me during the process. Thank you, honey, for your abiding love; it's the same as when we first met, if not a little more now. To my daughter, Hana, for keeping me strong. You are the reason I try to be a good person every day, to be the best example I can be for you.

To my mom and dad, for raising me to become the person I am, and my sisters Mina and Jina, for their unconditional love and friendship. My brother-in-law, who quietly supported us and helped my sister Mina during the hard times. My mother-in-law, Debbie, and Michael's stepfather, Rich

Reed, for their love and support and all of Debbie's research on North Korea. To Frank, Karen, Jenna, and Kimberly Saldate, for your love and for being there when Michael called. And to the rest of Michael's and my families.

My editor, Vanessa Mobley, who just had a baby, I am so delighted by your dedication to my story and how fully you put your heart into it. To David Drake, for your wisdom in how to publish this book. You are one of the reasons why I chose Random House. Tammy Blake, for working behind the scenes to promote the book; I know what it's like to work behind the scenes. Thank you, David Tran, for the vision of the cover that captured the story. And Jenna Ciongoli, for keeping me up to date as we finished work on the book. To Diane Salvatore, for believing that the story will inspire people and for your passion for the book. Thank you to Lisa Dickey, my collaborator, for helping me put my story together beautifully in such a short time. To Jill Stern, for listening intently and for all the reassurance. And to Colleen Rafferty at ZSH, for dealing with Michael and me calling all the time.

There are so many friends I need to thank. I know I won't get to everyone, but know that you're appreciated so much. Here are some names I want to mention:

Su-yean and Eun-kyoung, for sharing my journey for twenty years. My film department classmates at Seoul Institute of the Arts. Arirang, for opening my eyes in my early twenties. Kyoung-hee and Moon Kim, thank you for reaching out to

Michael. And to Yena, for being a big sister to Hana when you see her.

Sunny Kwon, thank you so much for helping with Hana while I was away; I can't express how important it was to me. Aaron Hull and his family, for coming by and staying with Michael. Melissa Lawton, for your love and encouragement. Sean Donovan, for your vigil speech letting the world know my mom is the most fashionable mom in the world. Annika Allison Mandel, for speaking for me at a vigil, and for baking cookies for Michael when he needed comfort. Ruth Rosenthal and Yogi Graham, who believed in me while we were working together at Current TV, I treasure your continuing friendship. To Nzingha Shakur, for your heart and for sending the much-needed Bible verse that carried me through the five months. Kathy Zembera, Holly Gibson, and Mike Shen, for your hearts and the time you gave in arranging the SF vigils. Grace and Bruce Kuk and their sons, Andrew and Eric, for providing dinner for all my friends after the AAU vigil. Thank you, Eric, for speaking at the vigil; I know it was tough. For the many close friends who helped and prayed for us: Caroline Kang, Kris Lee, Hyoek-jin Kim and his family, James Yang and his family, Steve Lee, LeNeac Weathersby, Daphne Lim and her family, Ho-chun Kang and his family, Mi-sook Lee and Jinny Cho, Larry and Joan Dahlstrom, Katie Harless, Lori Williams, Wilson Choi, Soo-wan Jang and Choon-seon Kim, Jeong-kyoo Choi. And to Annie and Sabina Yoon, for throwing a welcome-home party for me.

Ed Champion, your phone calls to Michael cheered him up; I think it went something like this: 4, 5, 6. . . . Min-sun Hwang, thank you for your care and concern and sharing your honest opinion with me. To You-na Maeng and Su-jung Seo, for their prayers and for keeping things calm at Young Ye Preschool for Hana. Teacher Tina Yi and Yea-jin Kim, for your extra attention in helping Hana get through the difficult time. Dr. Vicky Y. Shimoyama, for gentle treatment and keeping Hana healthy. To Min-jin Hong, Tiffany Kwon, Min-young Choi, Keiji and Ima Moore, for being good friends to Hana.

Thanks to our neighbors Susan Porche and Merrilyn Crouch, who make it hard for us to move and are such good friends (and to Puppy, who loves playing with Hana). And to our across-the-street neighbor Ellen, for offering her help. Neil Gumenick, thank you for literally calming my nerves.

Knowing that so many churches, brothers, and sisters all prayed for Laura and me is so encouraging. I want to let you know I definitely felt armor around me. I deeply appreciate all of your prayers. And if I forgot to put your name here, please forgive me: To Reality LA Pastor Tim Chaddick, Pastor Nick Tortorici, and the rest of the pastoral staff. Thank you for praying for us and answering Michael's calls every time—even at 12 A.M. on a particular Wednesday morning. Reality LA members who still pray for my family and me, we are grateful. Jenny Song and Sabrina Brooks, for volunteering to watch Hana whenever Michael needed help. Mike Hahn, thanks for being there for

Michael, hanging out with him, and still coming around and helping me and my family. Sidney and Mark Logan, for using all of your connections to help us. Sidney, you barely met Michael and you were making those phone calls for us.

Paul and Kristine Korver, for making meals for Michael and Hana. Elisabeth Ha, for bringing food and arranging baby-sitters for Hana. Rich and Ayumi Moore, for your prayers and friendship. Thank you Mark Hoshi for spreading the word about my situation to the Church.

Ecclesia LA, we miss you guys, and thanks for praying for us. Terry and Reese Coli, I know we don't get to see you as much as we would like, but thank you for your support and offering to help watch Hana. To Global Mission Church's Pastor Lee in Seoul and its members for praying for Laura and my safe return. Virginia Smotherland, Dan and Isabelle Quita, Temple Baptist Church and its members, and all the congregations who prayed for us. We felt your love. Rev. Jesse Jackson, thank you for getting involved, and for your efforts in trying to get us home.

To President Clinton's team: President Bill Clinton, John Podesta, Doug Band, David Straub, Roger Band, Justin Cooper, Min-ji Kwon, the U.S. Secret Service, pilots and travel crew; I will never forget your elated welcome when I got on the plane. I am very humbled by your mission. And thank you, Chelsea Clinton, for supporting us and asking your dad to go get us. Steve Bing, thank you for your kind donation allowing us to travel back home.

Thank you, President Obama, for your decision to bring us home. I am grateful to Secretary of State Hillary Clinton for helping us even when things were tense between the two countries. And sorry for Hana spilling water on your coffee table. Thank you to the White House and State Department, especially Linda McFadyen, for all your help in comforting Michael and for letting Hana and Michael stay at your house. Kurt Tong, I know you worked very hard to get us home; a lot of your work went unknown. Allison Hooker, for your continuing support. Stephen Bosworth, Kurt Campbell, Dan Cintron, Roberta Cooper, Maureen Cormack, Glyn Davies, Joseph Detrani, Daryl Hegendorfer, Sherri Holliday-Sklar, Sung Kim, Julie Kim-Johnson, Dan Larsen, John Merrill, Cheryl Mills, Jaime Oberlander, Johna Ohtagaki, Pamela Park, Amy Patel, Eric Richardson, Jennifer Roque, Ed Shin, Jim Steinberg, Jake Sullivan, Mark Tesone, the U.S. Bureau of Consular Affairs, Janice L. Jacobs, Michele Thoren Bond, Michelle Bernier-Toth, David J. Schwartz, the U.S. Embassy Beijing, Richard L. Buangan, Linda L. Donahue, Nancy W. Leou, Bridget Liam Weinstein, and the U.S. Consulate General Shenyang.

Ambassador Mats Foyer of Sweden and Johan Eidman, thank you for your endless efforts to see us while in North Korea and not leaving the DPRK until we got home. I can't express how much comfort I received from your visits. And thank you for printing all the letters and getting the boxes of supplies to us. I hope to see you again someday.

ACKNOWLEDGMENTS

At Current TV: Al Gore, for keeping your promise to bring us home, and thank you for giving Michael the Xbox 360 for a distraction; he still plays it. Joel Hyatt, for believing in your strategy and pursuit of it to bring us home. Joanna Drake Earl, for your concern for my situation and for comforting Michael. David Harleston, for your biggest hug for me. David Neuman, for your support for my family and your being welcoming even during your busiest days. And to Mark Rosenthal, for your support for my decisions.

The Vanguard Team: I can't thank you enough for your support and love and endless letters. Your letters were like a documentary of the outside world while I was isolated, and your selfless love for my family is something that I learned from. Whenever I pass by Shakey's, I think of you all and again feel humbled by working with such good people. Thank you, Darren and Yasu, for doing an awesome job filming Hana's graduation for me; I kept telling Michael that we got big-budget cameramen to film the ceremony. I may have missed the ceremony, but you saved it for me. Thanks to our awesome Vanguard team members: Adam Yamaguchi, Andrew McAllister, Benita Sills, Cerissa Tanner, Christof Putzel, Darren Foster, Jennifer Olivar, Joanne Shen, Kaj Larsen, Lauren Cerre, Mariana Van Zeller, Sean Puglisi, Tracey Chang, Tania Rashid, and Yasu Tsuji. Mitch Koss, thanks to your quick actions people were immediately aware of our situation. *Makeup artists:* Michelle Affronti, Julie Armstrong, and Jenna Keller, thanks for making Hana a princess whenever she visited the office. She loves princesses and I know she was delighted. She still asks me to take her to the office. *Studio team*: Michael DeHart, Michael Wardlow, Lew Abramson, Joe LaMonica, Brendon Clark, B-Love, Emily Foster, Emily Brown, Corinna Fisher, Kevin McLaughlin, Matt Donovan, Rawley Valverde, and the rest of the studio team who befriended Michael while he was with Current. *Super News crew*: Josh Faure-Brac, Steve Olson, Dustin McLean, Martin Carillo, Andre Nguyen, Paula Holmberg, Brian Shortall, Kevin Murray, Eli Goldstein, Bob Harper, Ken McEntire—you are the funniest group of people. Noreen Moustafa, for taking care of all the logistics for Michael. And thanks to the rest of the Current family.

To the people in the Korean community who prayed for us, thank you. And thank you for remembering our brothers and sisters to the north.

Chang Lee, I am sorry we never got to eat the mi-yok guk the day I arrived home, but I appreciate your caring nature. To all those who held vigils keeping our story alive: Brendon Creamer, you rallied so many people behind us with your Facebook mastery. I am happy that we became good friends. Teddy Zee, thanks for the encouragement when Laura and I came home. And for all of the support while we were gone. Welly Yang and Dina Morishita, thank you for organizing the L.A. vigil; I heard Wokcano was packed. Kevin Desoto, the new media video wiz. Champ Clark from *People*, for your understanding and for giving Michael the space he needed.

Rose Tibayan, thank you for organizing the Chicago vigils

and letting Michael stay at your place. Also, a shout-out of thanks to all who helped in Chicago. Linda Yu and Nancy Loo for your support, from behind the scenes, for the vigils. Elyssa Lee for speaking on behalf of my family at the Sacramento vigil. Elsa Cheung for your support. Stephanie Huang Tsai, Joe Omar Gonzalas, Kristina Velasco, Brenna Hamilton. Paula Rangel, thank you for the beautiful dolls. Hana loves them. Lynn Perkins, Rob Everett, Rebecca Delgado and Academy of Art University, Jim Jordan, Beth Diebels, Marcus Marquez, Meghan Miller Jedrezejczyk and the entire family, Jeff Ong, Mindy Lee, Lisa Anderson Ellett, Max Jones and Kim Jones, his mother, Asia Liu, Dan Beckmann, Karen Leigh, Danielle Chang, Janice Lee, Jami Floyd, and the people in France and South Korea. There are so many people who organized and attended vigils for us. Please forgive me if I did not mention your name.

Thanks to Reporters Without Borders, Amnesty International, the Committee to Protect Journalists, the Asian American Journalists Association, and the lauraandeuna.com team. It was a tough time to keep our story alive and you treated it as if it were your situation. I was told all journalists were behind us while I was in North Korea. What a big relief. Your efforts meant a lot to me.

Everyone who helped keep the focus on our situation: Alanna Zahn, thank you for volunteering your home to handle all of the media for my husband and daughter. Lauri Deason, Lisa Anderson, Alex Castro, Sharon Ito, George

Huang, Hugh Hung, Kelly Hu, you kept handing Michael a candle when his would go out. Takoa Statham, David Kater, Chris Pham, Bobby Choy, Tom Plate, Mia Kim, Michele Chan, Susie Suh, Mark Dacasascos, Nickie Shapira, Morgan Wandell, Diane Sawyer, Larry King, Margaret Aro, Jonathan Klein, Anderson Cooper, Clothilde Le Coz, Ron Burkle, President Jimmy Carter, Congressman Ed Royce, Congressman Dan Lungren, Governor Arnold Schwarzenegger, Governor Bill Richardson, Senator Dianne Feinstein, Senator Barbara Boxer, Supervisor Mike Antonovich, Congressman Howard Berman, Mayor Kevin Johnson, Assemblywoman Fiona Ma, Senator John Kerry, British Foreign Secretary David Milibrand, British Foreign Office Minister Bill Rammell, Baroness Janet Whitaker, Baroness Caroline Cox, Lord David Alton, Ambassador Peter Hughes, and the Korean Peninsula Desk at the British Foreign Commonwealth Office.

My grateful thanks to the Chopra family, whom my family did not know but now are friends with. Mallika Chopra for your nice blogs that kept our story alive and getting all of the moms involved. Gotham Chopra for keeping the story alive and talking trash about sports with Michael.

It is hard to take the time to write someone who is a total stranger, and many of you did not know me and yet you wrote me. I appreciate your love and concern for my family and me. Many different people from many different cities, states, and countries sent me letters and postcards. I put them up on the wall of my detainment room to show the North Korean authorities that America cares and that friends from around the world supported us. I am grateful for the words of encouragement from Ann Blackman and Michael Putzel, Gina and Mike Cerre, Tori Taylor McMillan, Emily Donelan, Joe Maidenberg, Malcolm and Jo Lee, James Abee, Gary Casazza, Stacy Pietrafitta, Angela Sun, Justin Kelly, Mei Chi, Bryan and Cheryl, Ann Song, Jean Roh, and Phil Hong. Thank you not only for your support but also for bringing Min Jin to play with Hana when she and Michael went to Iain's house.

Lauren Groux, Marc, Jen Birkey, Fred Baker, Andy Ta, Rachel Yee-Horvath, Allison Davis, Laura's Auntie Anna, Eric, David Casey, Mike Bunnell, Lynnette Brawer, Georgi Goldman, Sean Ludan, Jenn Wood, Mary and Ron and Luke, Ginny Jones, Dean Cooper, Savannah Moon, Lori Hoggatt, Josh S., Nathan Potter, Amy S., Pat, Maria, Jerrid and Katie Neal, Judy and Joe Rehfeld, Chelsey, Sarah Rickard, Janine Williams, Lori, EJ Cho, Bennett, Deborah Kim, Kevin Zeese, Kaytie Chow, Dan Ozborne, Janet Sniender, Margaret Morris, Becky Lockett, Kim Sare, Sparky, Sara Franks, Helen Revelette, Susan Finlayson, and many other people who sent me postcards and letters. . . .

I thank Laura's big family, who treated Michael and Hana as their own, especially Mary, Lisa, Paul, and Iain.

To Laura, even though we were separated, knowing you were there gave me strength and comfort, especially hearing your voice at the trial. . . . We went through so much together—I believe our bond is strong and tight.

And to the Lord Jesus, thank you for touching people's hearts to bring us home and for your strength to get my family and me through all of this.

About the Author

Euna Lee is a film editor for Current TV, a cable network co-founded by former vice president Al Gore. As an editor, she has worked on humanitarian stories such as the HIV/AIDS epidemic in India, American troops in Iraq, the U.S. war on drugs in Bolivia, and parolees in the United States. She was working as a producer on a documentary about North Korean defectors when she was arrested and detained in North Korea. She earned a Motion Pictures & Television degree at the Academy of Art University in San Francisco, and she lives in Los Angeles with her husband, Michael, and daughter, Hana.